AF803500

Routledge Revivals

The Physiology of Industry

The *Physiology of Industry* is a remarkable work which set out to challenge contemporary theory surrounding the economics of labour, supply and demand. First published in 1889, Hobson's first book outlines some of the key areas of his theory of underconsumption. The precise contribution of Mummery, who died in a mountaineering accident in 1895, is unclear, although Hobson did state that it was heated debates with the businessman that gave him faith in these theories. The chapters analyse the nature of production, the relationship between wealth and consumption, the influence of the supply of gold on the economy and the law of supply and demand. This is an interesting work which marked a shift in economic thought, and will be of value to researchers and student of industrial theory and modern economic history.

The Physiology of Industry

J.A. Hobson and A.F. Mummery

Routledge
Taylor & Francis Group
ROUTLEDGE REVIVALS

First published in 1889
Reprinted 1992
by Routledge/Thoemmes Press

This edition first published in 2013 by Routledge
2 Park Square, Milton Park, Abingdon, Oxon, OX14 4RN

Simultaneously published in the USA and Canada
by Routledge
711 Third Avenue, New York, NY 10017

Routledge is an imprint of the Taylor & Francis Group, an informa business

© 1992 Routledge/Thoemmes Press

All rights reserved. No part of this book may be reprinted or reproduced or utilised in any form or by any electronic, mechanical, or other means, now known or hereafter invented, including photocopying and recording, or in any information storage or retrieval system, without permission in writing from the publishers.

Publisher's Note
The publisher has gone to great lengths to ensure the quality of this reprint but points out that some imperfections in the original copies may be apparent.

Disclaimer
The publisher has made every effort to trace copyright holders and welcomes correspondence from those they have been unable to contact.

A Library of Congress record exists under LC control number: 94113062

ISBN 13: 978-0-415-82538-2 (hbk)
ISBN 13: 978-0-203-38374-2 (ebk)

J. A. HOBSON

A COLLECTION OF ECONOMIC WORKS

THOEMMES
REPRINTS

Printed in Great Britain by
Antony Rowe Ltd, Chippenham, Wiltshire

THE PHYSIOLOGY OF INDUSTRY

J.A. Hobson
and A.F. Mummery

With a new Introduction by
Roger E. Backhouse

ROUTLEDGE / THOEMMES PRESS

© 1992 Routledge / Thoemmes Press

Published in 1992 by
Routledge / Thoemmes Press
11 New Fetter Lane
London EC4P 4EE

Reprinted 2000

J.A. Hobson: A Collection of Economic Works
6 Volumes: ISBN 0 415 08304 4

This is a reprint of the 1889 Edition

Routledge / Thoemmes Press is a joint imprint
of Routledge and Thoemmes Antiquarian Books Ltd.

Publisher's Note

These reprints are taken from original copies of each book. In many cases the condition of those originals is not perfect, pages having suffered from such things as inconsistent printing pressures, show-through from one side of a leaf to the other, the filling in of some letters and characters, unstable, often handmade, paper and the break up of type. The publisher has gone to great lengths to ensure the quality of these reprints but points out that certain characteristics of the original copies will, of necessity, be apparent in reprints thereof.

INTRODUCTION

John Maynard Keynes, in his *General Theory* (1936), paid tribute to Hobson as one of the leading members of what he called a brave army of heretics that struggled against the Ricardian orthodoxy. *The Physiology of Industry*, published in 1889, Hobson's first book, contains his first exposition of this heresy. Though he refined his ideas in his later work by relating underconsumption to the concept of the unproductive surplus and his theory of imperialism, the key components of his theory of underconsumption are to be found in the *Physiology*. This book also contains other important theoretical contributions. The 'law of the limiting requisite' (chapter VI) is a coherent supply-and-demand theory of income distribution, in which capital and labour are treated symmetrically. When the assumption of fixed technical coefficients was replaced with that of variable factor proportions, the result was a marginal productivity theory of distribution (Hobson, 1891; 1900). Chapter VII contains a critique of the notion that falling prices were caused by a shortage of gold. This contains many of the ideas that Hobson later used in his critique of Irving Fisher's quantity theory of money (Hobson, 1913). Finally, mention should be made of the remarkably precise statement (pp. 85—6) of what later came to be called the acceleration principle, usually attributed to Carver (1903).

One of the puzzles surrounding the *Physiology* concerns the exact contribution of Hobson's co-author, A. F. Mummery. In *Confessions of an Economic*

Heretic Hobson states that it was long debates with Mummery, a businessman, that persuaded him of the truth of underconsumptionism. Hobson claims to have used all the orthodox arguments against Mummery, to no avail. Mummery, however, made no further contributions to economics, for he died in a mountaineering accident in 1895.

The orthodox view was that underconsumptionist arguments were fallacious. In the 1820s Ricardo and Malthus debated the question, with Malthus failing to make a coherent case for his claim that there could be a deficiency of demand. It was this debate which prompted Keynes to express the view that 'if only Malthus, instead of Ricardo, had been the parent stem from which 19th-century economics proceeded, what a much wiser and richer place the world would be today'. Though they refused to countenance the concept of underconsumptionism, orthodox economists, notably John Stuart Mill (1848) did acknowledge the possibility that a deficiency of demand might occur, but they minimized its importance. With only a few exceptions, such as Walker (see Backhouse, 1987), no-one sought to provide a theory of persistent depression. Hobson and Mummery (p. 102) point out that Marshall (1879) recognized that 'though men may have the power to purchase, they may choose not to use it', observing, quite correctly, that Marshall 'fails to grasp the critical importance of this fact, and appears to limit its action to periods of "crisis" '. What they do not notice, however, is that this was virtually a quotation from Mill (neither do they acknowledge that *The Economics of Industry* had a second author, Alfred Marshall's wife, Mary Paley Marshall).

Whilst academic economists minimized the importance of deficiences in aggregate demand, the same was not true of businessmen and trade uinionists. It is impossible to read the evidence presented to the Royal Commission on Depression in Trade and Industry (1886) without noticing the frequent, repeated expression of support for underconsumptionist ideas. It is hardly an exaggeration to say that amongst such people, underconsumption was the generally accepted cause of depression.

One of the explanations of this popularity of underconsumptionist ideas can easily be found in the experience of the 1870s and 1880s. There was a very strong boom in 1873, followed by an exceptionally deep and long-lasting recession in many countries. Though some countries, such as the United States, experienced a long period of very low production, the main feature of the depression was falling prices and low profits. In Britain the Royal Commission on Depression in Trade and Industry summarized the evidence presented to it in the following way:

> (a) the trade and industry of the country are in a condition which may be fairly described as depressed; (b) by this depression is meant a diminution, and in some cases, an absence of profit, with a corresponding diminution of employment for the labouring classes; (c) neither the volume of trade nor the amount of capital invested therein has materially fallen off, though the latter has in many cases depressed value; (d) the depression . . . dates from about the year 1875, and that with the exception of a short period of prosperity enjoyed by certain branches of trade in the years 1880 to 1883, it has proceeded with tolerable uniformity and has affected those branches which are connected with agriculture.

The theoretical framework underlying *The Physiology of Industry* reflects the transition which was taking place, during the 1870s and 1880s, from classical economics, of which the leading representative at this time was Mill's *Principles of Political Economy* (1848), and 'marginalist', or 'neoclassical' economics, built on works such as Jevons' *Theory of Political Economy* (1871). Classical economics was concerned above all with problems of economic growth, dealing with aggregates, and paying attention to the distribution of income between classes. In contrast the marginalist approach involved focusing on the decision-making of individual economic agents, with a shift in emphasis towards problems of resource allocation. Although marginalist ideas were, by 1889, becoming widely accepted, they were not securely established until the 1890s, and classical concepts and ways of approaching the subject were still widely adopted. Thus in the *Physiology* we find an emphasis on consumer demand as the source of demand for factors, and an endorsement of the perspective from which consumption is seen as pre-eminent. Hobson and Mummery argue that economists such as Jevons, Laveleye and Sidgwick recognized this, but did not take the argument to its logical conclusion. At the same time, their analysis of competition is almost classical, and they still take the wages fund as their target for attack. Their treatment of competition and of money reflects a background of classical economics.

According to the wages fund doctrine, it is the size of the wages fund (a stock of capital) which, given the wage rate, determines the level of demand for labour. It follows that an increase in consumption, other things being equal, reduces the demand for labour. Hobson and Mummery argue that, far from being undertaken at the expense of capital, consumption sustains the capital stock, for the demand for factors of production and for intermediate goods is derived from demand for consumption goods. They advocate, therefore, replacing the wages fund with the formula Production minus Saving equals Consumption (p. vii).

This stress on consumption as the source of demand for labour should not, however, be taken as implying a Keynesian view of the relation between saving, investment and employment. Like most economists writing before the 1920s, they view savings as automatically being invested.

> 'Saving means something more than this ['not consuming']. It signifies not only abstention from consumption, but application as a means of further production' (p. 47). 'No saving is effected unless the aggregate of capital is increased' (p. 103).

Problems of underconsumption arise precisely *because* savings are being invested. High savings lead to a high rate of capital accumulation, and hence to a rapid growth of supply relative to demand. Their theory is thus one in which overproduction arises because capital is accumulating so fast that demand for goods cannot keep up with potential supply. This argument is similar to the one Malthus (1820) used in his theory of gluts, and has more in common with the growth theory of Harrod (1939) and Domar (1946) than with Keynes's theory of unemployment. It is quite consistent with the view of the Royal Commission, cited above, that though its value had fallen, the amount of capital invested remained high.

Though the previous paragraph outlines the *Physiology*'s main theory of underconsumption, there are also passages where they argue that underconsumption may arise because individuals choose not to spend all their income. The result is an explanation of deficient demand not dissimilar to Mill's:

> 'The community considered as the recipient of money incomes produces consumable articles; the com-

> munity considered as the spender of money incomes buys and consumes these articles. If, owing to its desire to save, it refrains from spending the whole of its money income, the whole of the consumable articles produced cannot be sold. Over-supply is, in consequence, caused, and prices and incomes continually fall until the production of consumable articles is reduced to the total actually consumed' (pp. 98—9).

Later on in the book there is an interesting passage where Mummery and Hobson refer to the role of bankers in this process, suggesting that banks may, albeit temporarily, offset a shortage of saving by increasing their lending. They start by assuming that consumption falls, and savers cease to invest in industry, choosing instead to deposit their savings with banks (*i.e.* a fall in consumption accompanied by a rise in liquidity preference). Bankers may, for a while, continue to advance sufficient funds to enable producers to maintain their production levels, but such relief cannot be permanent. Eventually banks will become unwilling to increase their lending, and firms will be forced to sell surplus stocks: prices will fall and depression will ensue. This, they argue, is what happened after 1873.

Hobson and Mummery were clearly familiar with the circular flow of income. What was missing from their work, and was missing from all writing before the 1920s, was the concept of the multiplier. This is illustrated in their discussion of the relationship between money and income. In a manner reminiscent of 18th-century writers such as Cantillon and Hume, Hobson and Mummery focus on the income generated by an inflow of money. They argue that a gold inflow of £2m. per year will raise aggregate demand by £2m. per year. They compared this figure (which corresponded to the alleged fall in gold production) with the level of national income, and concluded that it could account for but a fraction of the 30% fall in prices between 1873 and 1885.

The problem with their analysis of money was that, like many of the classical economists, they had no concept of the demand for a stock, whether of money or any other asset. Demand for money was viewed as demand for a flow. They thus failed to see the point, crucial to an understanding of the quantity theory, that there could be an imbalance between the stock of money and the quantity people wished to hold. Hobson's *Gold, Prices and Wages* (1913), even though it was written after Fisher's *The Purchasing Power of Money* (1911), exhibited the same blind spot.

Throughout the book Hobson and Mummery assume a fixed relationship between what they term the 'requisites of production', capital and labour. When considering distribution they make the assumptions that for each factor there is a minimum price below which supply will be zero. The assumption of fixed coefficients means that there will, in general, be a surplus of one factor or the other. Competition, they argue, means that the surplus factor will receive only the necessary minimum supply price, with the residual going to the scarce factor, the 'limiting requisite'. The assumption of fixed coefficients leads to what seems, to economists familiar with marginal productivity theory, an unusual theory of distribution, but is quite consistent, and requires only the assumption of variable factor proportions to transform it into a marginal productivity theory.

Hobson and Mummery pointed out that the relationship between consumption and capital had a time dimension. Production takes time, which means that it is the prospect of future consumption that sustains the present capital stock. They were thus led to a perceptive analysis of underconsumption in terms of an inter-temporal disequilibrium. Their analysis of this problem has much to commend it, their statement of the acceleration principle being particularly noteworthy. Their main failing was probably their failure to grasp the notion of the demand for a stock, for this led not only to their failure to understand the quantity theory properly, but, perhaps more critically, to their failure to integrate their theory of money with their theory of deficient demand. The links between saving, hoarding and the demand for money were never clarified. Despite these problems, however, *The Physiology of Industry* was a remarkable book which, in Keynes's words, marked an epoch in economic thought.

Roger E. Backhouse
University of Birmingham, 1992

References

Backhouse, R. E. (1987) 'F. A. Walker's theory of "hard times"', *History of Political Economy* 19(3), 435—46.

——— (1990) 'J. A. Hobson as a macroeconomic theorist', in M. Freeden (ed.) *Reappraising J. A. Hobson*. London: Unwin Hyman.

Carver, T. N. (1903) 'A suggestion for a theory of industrial depressions', *Quarterly Journal of Economics* 17, 497 ff.

Domar, E. (1946) 'Capital expansion, rate of growth and employment', *Econometrica* 14, 137—47.

Fisher, I. (1911) *The Purchasing Power of Money*. New York: Macmillan.

Great Britain, Royal Commission on Depression on Trade and Industry (1886), *First Report*, Cmnd. 4621; *Second Report*, Cmnd. 4715; *Third Report*, Cmnd. 4797; *Final Report*, Cmnd. 4893.

Harrod, R. F. (1939) 'An essay in dynamic theory', *Economic Journal* 49, 15—33.

Hobson, J. A. (1891) 'The law of the three rents', *Quarterly Journal of Economics* 5, 263 ff. Reprinted in *Essays on Distribution and Welfare*, London: Routledge/Thoemmes Press, 1992.

——— (1900) *The Economics of Distribution*. New York: Macmillan. Reprinted Clifton, N.J.: Augustus M. Kelley, 1972.

Hobson, J. A. (1913) *Gold, Prices and Wages*. London: Methuen. Reprinted, New York: Augustus M. Kelley, 1973.

——— (1938) *Confessions of an Economic Heretic*. London.

Jevons, W. S. (1871) *The Theory of Political Economy*. London: Macmillan.

Keynes, J. M. (1936) *The General Theory of Employment, Interest and Money*. London: Macmillan.

Malthus, T. R. (1820) *Principles of Political Economy*. London.

Marshall, A., and Marshall, M. P. (1879) *The Economics of Industry*. London: Macmillan.

Mill, J. S. (1848) *Principles of Political Economy*. London.

THE

PHYSIOLOGY OF INDUSTRY:

BEING AN EXPOSURE OF
CERTAIN FALLACIES IN EXISTING THEORIES
OF ECONOMICS.

By A. F. MUMMERY

AND

J. A. HOBSON.

PREFACE.

THE theory of Political Economy, as it left the hands of Mill some forty years ago, has received many vigorous assaults, and few economists can now be found who would consent to accept it as their creed; but, strangely enough, while essential links in the argument have been destroyed, the main practical conclusion to which it leads is still regarded as a truth which no one must question. This conclusion is stated by Mill in these words, 'saving enriches and spending impoverishes the community along with the individual,' and it may be generally defined as an assertion that the effective love of money is the root of all economic good. Not merely does it enrich the thrifty individual himself, but it raises wages, gives work to the unemployed, and scatters blessings on every side. From the daily papers to the latest economic treatise, from the pulpit to the House of Commons, this conclusion is reiterated and re-stated till it appears positively impious to question it. Yet the educated world, supported by the majority of economic thinkers, up to the publication of Ricardo's work strenuously denied this doctrine, and its ultimate acceptance was exclusively due to their inability to meet the now exploded wages-fund doctrine. That the conclusion should have survived the argument on which it logically stood, can be explained on no other hypothesis than the commanding authority of the great men who asserted it. Economic critics have ventured to attack the theory in detail, but they have shrunk appalled from touching its main conclusions. Our purpose is to show that these conclusions are not tenable, that an undue exercise of the habit of saving is possible, and that such undue exercise impoverishes the Community, throws labourers out of work, drives down wages, and spreads that gloom and prostration through the commercial world which is known as Depression in Trade; that, in short, the effective love of money is the root of all economic evil. Having thus stated the conclusions to which our argument leads, it appears desirable to give a brief outline of its course, and to note the more important points at which it conflicts with currently accepted dogmas.

The object of production is to provide 'utilities and conveniences' for consumers, and the process is a continuous one from the first handling of the raw material to the moment when it is finally consumed as a utility or a convenience. The only use of Capital being to aid the production of these utilities and conveniences, the total used will necessarily vary with the total of utilities and conveniences daily or weekly consumed. Now saving, while it increases the existing aggregate of Capital, simultaneously reduces the quantity of utilities and conveniences consumed; any undue exercise of this habit must, therefore, cause an accumulation of Capital in excess of that which is required for use, and this excess will exist in the form of general over-production.

Examining the terms Demand and Supply, and extending Professor Cairnes' argument on this subject, we reach a law of price which enables us to relate our theory to existing commercial phenomena, and to identify Depression in Trade with a general fall in the rate of incomes; this latter with a decrease in the quantity of the use of the Requisites of Production demanded relatively to the quantity available for use; and this, again, with insufficiency in the quantity of utilities and conveniences demanded, an insufficiency which we show can only arise from the unduly saving habits of the Community. We are thus brought to the conclusion that the basis on which all economic teaching since Adam Smith has stood, viz., that the quantity annually produced is determined by the aggregates of Natural Agents, Capital, and Labour available, is erroneous, and that, on the contrary, the quantity produced, while it can never exceed the limits imposed by these aggregates, may be, and actually is, reduced far below this maximum by the check that undue saving and the consequent accumulation of over-supply exerts on production; *i.e.*, that in the normal state of modern industrial Communities, consumption limits production and not production consumption. We illustrate the effect of this check, step by step, by the commercial phenomena of the years immediately succeeding 1870.

We then trace the economic laws determining the distribution of the annual income amongst Natural Agent, Labour, and Capital owners, and show that the present rate of wages would be considerably higher were it not for the undue thrift of the richer members of the Community, and the consequent continuous and persistent over-supply.

Our first point of divergence from the orthodox school is thus to be found in our refutation of the doctrine that saving does not reduce the aggregate consumed, but merely varies the consumers. We show this doctrine to be founded on the wages-fund theory, and we demonstrate that it is not tenable and must be replaced by the simple formula—

$$\text{Production} - \text{Saving} = \text{Consumption};$$

i.e., the aggregate of Production being given every increase in saving diminishes by its exact total the aggregate consumed.

Showing that the use of Natural Agents, Labour, and Capital, creates utilities and conveniences, we are able to prove that the money paid for these utilities and conveniences is paid for the use of the Natural Agents, Labour, and Capital concerned, and that the quantity of such use demanded is determined by the quantity of these utilities and conveniences consumed. We are, in consequence, at issue with that school of economists who assert that "Demand for Commodities" (utilities and conveniences) "is not Demand for Labour."

Reaching our main conclusion, that the undue saving of individuals impoverishes the Community, simultaneously lowering Rent, Profit, or Interest and Wages, we contradict the generally accepted dogmas that the saving of the individual must always and necessarily enrich the Community, that the individual seeking his own advantage necessarily works for that of the Community, and that wages can only rise at the expense of profit, or profit at the expense of wages, or both at the expense of rent.

In Chapter VII. we examine the contention of the currency school, that Depression in Trade is due either to insufficiency in the quantity of gold in existence, or to an increase in the cost of producing it, and we show that this theory is absolutely untenable. In the last chapter we glance briefly at some of the practical conclusions to which our theory leads, and note how effectual combination amongst labourers would enable them to very materially improve their position, a theoretic conclusion which has received some slight practical illustration by the recent action taken by labour combinations in various parts of this country. We also note that the charge of commercial imbecility, so freely launched by orthodox economists against our American cousins and other Protectionist Communities, can no longer be maintained by any of the Free trade arguments hitherto adduced, since all these are based on the assumption that over-supply is impossible.

In order to render our main argument easier to follow we have carefully excised minor qualifications, reservations, and explanations, and though this doubtless exposes us to misconstruction and adverse criticism on minor details, we think this disadvantage more than balanced by the greater clearness with which it enables us to present our theory as a whole.

With the same object in view, we have placed, after the table of contents, a series of definitions which will enable our readers to easily and at once ascertain the exact meaning which is to be attributed to the terms employed.

Contents.

CHAPTER I.

Scope of Production.

CHAPTER II.

Quantitative Relation of Wealth to Consumption.

CHAPTER III.

The Physiology of Production.—The Law of Supply and Demand.

CHAPTER IV.

Over-Production and Economic Checks.

CHAPTER V.

Expansion and Contraction of Trade.

CHAPTER VI.

The Law of the Limiting Requisite.

CHAPTER VII

Scarcity of Gold as an Economic Factor.

CHAPTER VIII.

PRACTICAL CONSIDERATIONS.

Definitions.

PRODUCTION is the work of endowing material or immaterial forms with Exchange Value.

PRODUCERS are those engaged in the work of Production, and are divisible into two classes:—

I. MAKERS (Agriculturists, Manufacturers, and all who create Value by changing Shape).

II. TRADERS (Merchants, Wholesale or Retail Vendors, and all who create Value by changing Place).

REQUISITES OF PRODUCTION are those instruments which, by their Use, contribute to the work of Production. They are three in number: Natural Agents, Capital, Labour. [Capital includes all Plant, Raw Material, and articles embodying value which have not yet reached their final destination.]

CONSUMPTION is the sudden or gradual destruction of a valuable article obtained from a retail trader or other final producer.

CONSUMERS are those who obtain possession of valuable articles in order to destroy them for the direct satisfaction of their own desires; *i.e.*, not as a means to producing other things.

COMMODITIES are valuable articles in the possession of (or in the act of passing into the possession of) Consumers.

GOODS are valuable articles in the various stages of production between Raw Material and Commodity. Goods in the hands of Retailers are Shop-goods.

RENT is the payment for the Use of Natural Agents paid to their owner.

PROFIT is the payment for the Use of Capital paid to its owner. The Profit or payment for the Use of Money is called Interest.

WAGES are the payment for the Use of the bodily or mental Abilities of the Labourer; this use is termed Labour.

QUANTITY DEMANDED is—

(1.) In relation to an Individual or a Class—the quantity bought by such individual or class.

(2.) In relation to the Community—the quantity bought by Consumers.

QUANTITY SUPPLIED is identical with Quantity Demanded, regarded from the point of view of the Selling Individual, Class, or Community

DEMAND is the quantity of money paid for the Quantity Demanded.

SUPPLY is—

(1.) In relation to an Individual or a Class—the quantity of articles offered for Sale by such individual or class.

(2.) In relation to the Community—the aggregate of articles available for Sale to Consumers.

MONEY INCOME (Income)—

(1.) Of the Individual—is the excess of money values possessed by him at the end of the year, plus the money spent during the year, over the sum of money values possessed by him at the beginning of the year.

(2.) Of the Community--the aggregate of the Money Incomes of all individuals in the Community.

REAL INCOME—

(1.) Of the Individual—is that portion of the stock of wealth of the Community which his money income would purchase.

(2.) Of the Community—is the total wealth consumed during the year, plus any increase in Capital.

CHAPTER I.

THE SCOPE OF PRODUCTION.

SINCE the science of economics is concerned with matters which engross the thoughts and conversation of the large mass of unscientific men, special heed is required in the adoption and use of those common terms current in the world of commerce. In no other realm of knowledge have 'masked words' wrought such confusion: the name 'idols of the market' has a peculiar fitness when applied to those loose and deceptive commercial phrases the unmasking of which has formed the chief occupation of economic thinkers. Even now it is impossible to approach the study without perceiving the entrance beset with terms and phrases respecting the use of which nearly all previous writers are at variance, and which each separate writer finds it hard to employ for any long argument without unconsciously shifting the sense.

The production, the distribution, and the exchange of wealth are the three objects of investigation which most modern writers[1] set before them; others, and generally the older economists, add the term consumption.

[1] *E.g.*, Mill, 'Principles of Pol. Econ.,' p. 14; Fawcett, Book I., Ch. I.; Sidgwick, Ch. II.

Now the setting forth on an equal footing of these three or four objects of consideration, and the attempt at a separate treatment of them, have been a fruitful source of confusion not only to the readers but to the writers of economic treatises.

The loose use of the word distribution has caused the most trouble. Following the term production, and used in close association with the term exchange, it would naturally suggest the work or process whereby the products which had received their final shape were conveyed from the place where they were manufactured in order to be retailed to the final consumers. This meaning would easily accommodate itself to the general use of the term production, which is confined to the transmutation and transformation of material objects, and does not include their conveyance to the place where they are wanted. Now, though writers like Mill and Fawcett do not go so far as to directly authorise this extremely narrow use of the term production, they do distinctly represent distribution as a process which follows the process of production, and furnishes employment for certain classes of labourers. Thus Mill, in the very chapter[1] where he is treating of labour as an agent in production, expressly distinguishes the producing class from the distributing class, including under the latter all "dealers and traders." The 'class of labourers employed in rendering the things produced accessible' are styled by him 'distributors.' It is clear, then, that with him the work of production ends when the products are stored in the factory in a completed shape, and that the work of distribution then begins.

[1] 'Principles of Pol. Econ.,' Book I., Ch. II., s. 6.

Mill further[1] regards exchange as "the instrumentality by which distribution is effected," thus emphasising his view of distribution as a process following production. Although Fawcett does not follow Mill in narrowing the producing class so as to exclude traders and retailers when dealing specifically with this question, he allows himself later on to distinguish the work of exchange and of distribution from that of production. "It is quite true," he says,[2] "that commodities are only produced to be exchanged for other commodities, and the distribution of wealth, of course, implies the exchange of wealth." It is clear that he here falls into the same narrow use of production which Mill authorises. Many other passages might be quoted to show how economists have allowed themselves to be misled by the common use of the term distribution as a process contrasted with the process of production.[3] It is only fair to say, however, that neither Mill nor Fawcett, when they have come to the consideration

[1] 'Pol. Econ.,' Book II., Ch. XVI., s. 6; and Book III., Ch. I., s. 1.

[2] Book III., Ch. I.

[3] Marshall, Book II., Ch. VI., s. 1, and Sidgwick, p. 171, escape this confusion. Prof. Sidgwick, however, does not realise the extent of the trouble caused by the confusion, and he himself uses ambiguous language in speaking of 'division of aggregate produce' as the object of distribution. Distribution, as a branch of economics, has nothing to do with the commercial process of division, but only, as Prof. Sidgwick himself points out (p. 175), with the 'laws,' according to which 'the increment of new commodities is shared among the different classes of persons' who have 'co-operated in providing it.' He, however, appears to include under the forms of wealth with the division of which 'distribution' is concerned, 'additions to industrial capital.' The laws of distribution are rightly concerned only with the apportionment of what Prof. Sidgwick terms 'consumers' wealth,' which will be found to be the sole source of the real income of the community.

of distribution, have dealt with it as a process subsequent to production. The questions they there propound and discuss have no relation to the process of distributing or the means of distribution, but relate exclusively to the principles which regulate the proportion of the created utilities which falls to the respective parties who have assisted to produce them. Since it is clear that to this final apportionment distribution alone rightly refers, it is a great misfortune that a term should have been selected to express it which has been able to deceive the very elect.

We have already noted the tendency in Fawcett [1] to make of exchange another process separate from production, although in his discussion of the agents of production he would include all those engaged in the work of exchange. The same tendency, induced by an unconscious adherence to the vulgar, narrow use of production, may be observed in the writings of other economists. For example, in Mr. Amasa Walker's able manual, 'Science of Wealth' (p. 36), after dealing with "production of wealth," the author proceeds: "Since men have different capacities and tastes, their products will be different; and yet since all men desire nearly the same objects, an interchange of their respective commodities will become a necessity. Hence arises *that department of industry called exchange.*" Thus we see production and exchange as two separate 'departments of industry.' That the ordinary man of business should distinguish production, distribution, and exchange as three processes involving a separate machinery for each, is no

[1] *E.g.*, Book I., Ch. III.

matter of surprise, though even he must find some difficulty in distinguishing the machinery of distribution from the machinery of exchange. But that professed economists should have sanctioned this commercial division is extremely regretable, involving as it does a loose and inadequate idea of the unity of production.

What is production? involves the further question, What is produced? The answer is, value—exchange value. The whole work or process of producing value is termed production. Dealing for the present exclusively with the outer world of matter we next ask, How is value given to matter? By change of form or place. By change of form man gives value to agricultural or manufactured goods; he adds further value by moving them to the place where they are most wanted. The value thus created by the work of production must be regarded as an attribute bestowed upon and resident in the matter. Thus matter continually gathers value as it passes from the condition of raw material towards the condition of a utility, each step in the process adding to this value. The material does not cease accumulating value when it is turned out of the factory in a so-called finished state. The merchants, wholesale dealers, and shopkeepers through whose hands it passes afterwards on its way to the consumer, are distinct contributors to its final value equally with those whose work gave it a finished shape. In the one case, it acquires value by changing shape; in the other, by changing place. The latter value, just as the former, must be reckoned as value inherent in the article, even as it is found fully represented in the money price. Now all this, of course, no recent economist would straightly deny, but most of them by narrowing their use of the terms production and producer so as to exclude traders and shopkeepers, have implicitly denied it, and have lent themselves on this account to a fallacy subtler, and therefore perhaps even more disastrous than the mercantile theory which gave the earlier economists such pains.

Although it is obvious that the end of production is to supply "necessaries and conveniences of life"[1] to consumers, this end, consumption, has been lost sight of by almost all economic writers, who content themselves with a merely formal recognition of the place which consumption occupies in the economic system. Mill and Fawcett consider that political economy is concerned with the production, distribution, and exchange of wealth, apparently considering that labour has fully attained its end in producing articles which are distributed and exchanged.[2]

Other writers give a formal prominence to the element of consumption, which leads one to expect a systematic treatment of the subject. Professor Jevons went so far as to say that "the whole theory of economics must begin with a correct theory of consumption."[3] The words of Laveleye are even more significant: "The aim of production is the consumption of its products in the satisfaction of rational wants. Consumption is thus essential to production

[1] 'Wealth of Nations,' Introduction, p. 1.

[2] The only use they have for the term consumption is to found a theory of capital upon a generic distinction in the method of consumption. This theory we discuss at length later on.

[3] Jevons, 'Theory of Pol. Econ.,' Ch. II., p. 43.

and the final cause of all economic activity."[1] Professor Sidgwick announces in an early place in his book[2] that his inquiry will deal with "the general facts of the consumption of wealth so far as these are associated with the former," *i.e.*, with "production, distribution, and exchange." But the questions of consumption with which these writers are concerned deal with the wisdom or the folly, the pleasure and the pain, the net advantages and disadvantages of different kinds of consumption: they blend ethical and psychological considerations with economics, discussing the quality of consumption to the entire neglect of quantitative considerations.[3] In their insistence on the right use of wealth these authors give much sound ethical advice, though none of them points his moral so skilfully as Ruskin, who defines wealth as "a supply of really useful things for those who can use them;" if the things are not really useful or fall into wrong hands they cease to be wealth and become "illth."[4]

This utter neglect of the question of a quantitative relation between production and consumption, together with an inadequate grasp of the full meaning of production, has led economists to give their authority to the common impression that the real end of commerce is to produce the largest amount of goods in a finished shape, and that therein consists the real guarantee of commercial prosperity. The

[1] Laveleye, 'Pol. Econ.,' p. 246.

[2] 'Principles of Pol. Econ.,' p. 30.

[3] Laveleye attempts to deal very briefly with the quantitative relation between production and consumption. His argument is stated below.

[4] 'Unto this Last,' p. 126.

largest rate of production by means of a well-adjusted co-operation of capital and labour, is the goal to which they can point, and production means the process which is the necessary antecedent of distribution and exchange. They thus emphasise the value which is bestowed on raw material by the work which changes its shape, but neglect the value bestowed on it by the work which changes its place.

The uneducated mind may be excused for realising better the value which is accompanied by change in physical appearance than that which is accompanied by no such alteration, but the economist trained to the recognition of seen and unseen results can claim no such allowance. Yet the whole tendency of their teaching is to represent the production of a piece of finished goods as the end or completion of an act. When they have thus produced their wealth they pause, and afterwards proceed to the separate inquiry of how it shall be exchanged and distributed. Just as the mercantile theory made the acquisition of 'treasure' the test and measure of national commerce, so our modern economists have practically raised finished goods into the same position. Their fallacy is at bottom the same. We hear quite enough in elementary text-books of the bag of gold which Robinson Crusoe found. Yet in pressing the moral that the bag of gold was no wealth to the worthy mariner because he had no use for it, they neglect to drive home the deeper lesson that it is the use of all forms of wealth which enables them to reach their end. A finished piece of goods before it is 'exchanged and distributed' is no more a 'utility' or a 'convenience' than was Crusoe's gold. But why dwell on this point, which everyone is ready to recognise? Because economists by narrowing and obscuring the meaning of production have lost the idea of the essential unity of the process. What we, on the other hand, wish to enforce is this, that the process by which a piece of raw material becomes a useful commodity is one process; that the raw material gathers value continuously by work done upon it, not up to the time when it is said to be 'produced,' but up to the time when it is handed over to the consumer. The term production should and must rightly apply to the whole process, the wholesale merchant and the shopkeeper are just as rightly termed producers as the farmer or the manufacturer. This failure to clearly recognise that a commodity is being produced until it is consumed, this tendency to split up the history of its growth into several processes, are the reasons why economists have so lamentably failed to grasp and represent the entirety and the unity of the mechanism of commerce.

So far as the history of commodities is concerned there are but two phases. Commodities are produced and are consumed. There is no separate act of distribution which figures in their lives. Even the act of handing them over the counter to a purchaser is, strictly speaking, nothing but the final act in their production, is represented in their final value and paid for in their price. The laws of distribution, to use the unfortunate economic term, relate exclusively to the separate questions, Who shall consume? and In what proportion? and are concerned not directly with the apportionment of commodities but of purchasing power.

The laws of distribution thus regard the principles which regulate the proportion of command over final products which falls to the various agents in production, landlord, capitalist, labourer. If the proportion which holds to-day were changed to-morrow, so that labour received twice what it does at present and capital only half, the so-called 'work of distribution' would not necessarily be affected; the change might only mean that the same set of purchases will be made by a different set of persons. If we were to retain the term distribution for the work done by merchants and retailers, we should be obliged to distinguish the laws of production and of distribution as follows:—

The laws of production relate to the method of the work of production; the laws of distribution relate not to the method of the work of distribution, but to the final distribution of the produce. But this course would cause the direst confusion in dealing with facts of commerce, so that it will be found better, if possible, to dispense entirely with the term distribution in the analysis of commercial phenomena.

Regarding political economy, then, as the science which deals with the method of furnishing 'necessaries and conveniences' to the community, we find that it is concerned with three chief facts[1]:—

[1] These three economic facts will be found to be generally related in the following way:—When any value is created a general power to purchase to an equivalent extent is portioned out amongst those who have helped to create this value (with the equity of this apportionment we are not here concerned). This general power of purchase may be or may not be at once exercised. The results of its exercise or non-exercise are facts which fall under the head of consumption.

Production of necessaries and conveniences (including all the work of transportation and arrangement for the convenience of expected purchasers, commonly termed work of exchange and distribution).

Apportionment of power to purchase these necessaries and conveniences.

Consumption, or the use made of the power to purchase.

The first step in political economy is to establish a clear recognition of the unity of commerce in the work of production, the lack of which has caused such grave trouble in economic writing. To do this we will briefly trace the history of the production of a 'utility' from its first beginning to its final state. In this history we need take no account of the second of the three elements, apportionment of power to purchase, since we have already seen that it has no place in the history of a commodity. Consumption, as the final goal towards which production moves, requires a recognition in the history of a utility, but only as serving to furnish a mark for measuring the progress of the work of production. A favourite example with writers on economics is a pair of shoes, presumably because they are formed from a single raw material, instead of requiring a combination of different materials partly wrought. Now the raw material of a pair of shoes is the hide of live cattle, and the first producer of the shoes must be considered to be the butcher who purchases and kills the cattle; by these preliminary acts he has imparted a value to the hide which it did not possess when it was a part of the live animal. Then comes the tanner, who purchases the hide from the butcher and treats it, adding a further element of value. Then the shoe manufacturer, who puts it through various processes, each one of which adds distinctly to its value, and turns it out a finished pair of shoes so far as shape is concerned. But this pair of shoes is not yet either a utility or a convenience, lying, as it does, amid a pile of other shoes in a factory. A wholesale merchant buys it with a quantity of others and sells it again to a small retailer ; by doing this he adds to its value, bringing it nearer to the reach of a would-be purchaser. The small retail shopkeeper keeps it, displays it, and finally wraps it up, and hands it over the counter to a purchaser ; thus imparting to the pair of shoes their final element of value, he is rightly to be esteemed the last producer of the pair of shoes. The shopkeeper is the man who by his labour exercised on the shoes assists them to take the final step which makes them a 'utility or convenience.' Continuously through the whole progress we have described, the raw material has been gathering value by change of form or change of place ; the attainment of its full value is simultaneous with the grasp of the purchaser. The work of production has now reached its end, the work of consumption begins. Now it is absolutely essential that we should have some term to distinguish the article in the hands of a consumer, having already attained its full value, from the article in the process of acquiring this value and approaching this state. It is required to distinguish the pair of shoes in the hands of a purchaser, in the first place from a pair of shoes in the factory, in the second place from the shoemaking machinery which is not destined for consumption as a personal 'utility or convenience.'

Now there is no term set apart either by economics or by popular usage for this purpose. As it is deemed objectionable to invent terms, we are driven to the alternative of selecting some existing term, and restricting its use to suit our purpose. Etymological accuracy suggests the word commodity as being fit to represent an article which is in the hands of a consumer as a personal utility or convenience. We propose, therefore, to use the term commodity exclusively in this sense.[1] Raw material which has reached its final shape (*e.g.*, a pair of shoes after passing through the shoemaking processes) we shall term goods; goods in the hands of retailers we shall term shop-goods. This distinction, artificial as it sounds, is essential to the exposition of our theory of commerce. The history of a commodity expressed in these terms, then, will consist of a series of continuous steps, leading from raw material to goods, from goods to shop-goods, from shop-goods to commodities. The number of steps which lie between raw material and goods of course differs widely in different cases, as also the number of steps between goods and shop-goods. Again, in taking the history of a pair of shoes, we have assumed that each productive step in the progress from raw material (hide) to goods (shoes) has been registered in a change of shape of the material. This,

[1] Prof. Sidgwick uses the terms 'consumers' wealth' and 'producers' wealth' to make this same distinction between the wealth which is 'directly available for satisfying human wants and desires,' and the wealth which is 'useful indirectly as a means of obtaining the other.' (Principles of 'Pol. Econ.,' p. 86.) He does not, however, sharply mark the limits of the two classes by a definition of the term 'directly available' in such a way as to exclude everything not actually in the hands of consumers.

however, is not always so. The hides may be bought by a hide merchant who does not treat the hides himself, but sells them to the tanner. So, too, the finished leather may pass through a merchant's hands, receiving no change of shape before it enters the shoe-factory. Thus, productive operations which give change of place to material may be sandwiched in between the operations which change its shape from raw material to finished goods. To make the historic process clear we may mark the various steps or stages in the development of a commodity as follows, using the abbreviation R. M. for raw material, R. M.^{1} for the first stage in production, and so on.

R. M. . . . (Hide on cattle).
R. M.^{1} . . (Raw hides).
R. M.^{2} . . (Prepared hides).
R. M.^{3} . . (Leather).
Goods . . (Shoes).
G.^{1} . . . . (Shoes in exporter's hands).
G.^{2} . . . . (Shoes in merchant's hands).
Shop G. . (Shoes in shop).
Com. . . . (Shoes in use).

There may have been one or more intermediate step between R. M.^{1} and R. M.^{2}, or between R. M.^{2} and R. M.^{3}, or, indeed, at any point in the history of production of the commodity. In the particular commodity we selected, a pair of shoes, the work of change of shape for the most part precedes the work of change of place; but in the history of other commodities it is different. If we took the history of a loaf of bread, the steps of production which consist in change of place will be found almost to alternate with those steps which consist in change of shape.

The merchant's work, or, more generally speaking, the work of transportation, here may come in after the grain is produced, after it has been ground into flour, after the flour has been made into bread. Thus the history of a loaf of bread will present often a larger number of distinct steps than those which we have traced in the case of a pair of shoes. In other cases the steps are much fewer, and are not infrequently performed by the work of a single man, as where our supply of milk for household use is furnished directly by the farmer.

Although an explicit declaration of our intention to confine the term commodities to the sum of those 'utilities and conveniences' to provide which is acknowledged to be the sole end of commerce, might seem a sufficient definition, it will, perhaps, be wiser to guard against confusion by a further statement of what commodity includes.

While in one way we are narrowing the common use of the word, in another way we are assigning it a wider meaning. We are narrowing it in so far as we apply it only to that portion of material wealth which is in the hands of persons who use or consume it for their own benefit or pleasure, thus excluding not only raw material in its several stages, but also finished goods in warehouse or shop, and all plant and machinery used to forward production. Thus, neither a piece of leather, a pair of boots in a shop, or a last is a commodity. On the other hand, we are extending the meaning of the term to cover those utilities and conveniences which consist in services rendered by other persons, or by material objects belonging to other persons, in return for pay. Thus the song of an opera singer and the advice of a physician will be included under the head of commodities, as also the transmission of a letter for which we pay a penny stamp.

It must, however, be frankly acknowledged that this extension of the term commodity to include those non-material utilities and conveniences commonly called 'services,' though absolutely essential to a full understanding of the whole productive system, involves many difficulties, and affords ample scope for the exercise of casuistic criticism. For instance, it may be urged that as we would include conveyance in a hired carriage as a commodity, so we must include conveyance in our own private carriage under the same head; it will then follow that a private carriage is not itself a commodity, but only a machine producing the commodity 'conveyance,' unless we admit that one commodity can produce another. So, too, as a hired house is to be regarded as an instrument producing a commodity shelter, for which we pay the purchase-money rent, our own house should not be regarded as a commodity. But if our house is not a commodity, but only an instrument or machine continually producing a commodity shelter, might we not in like manner regard our clothes as an instrument producing the commodities warmth, decency, ornament, &c.? Thus we should be driven to admit that even food was not a commodity, but only the producer of a commodity, satisfaction of hunger, pleasure of taste, &c. The difficulties all spring from the fact that it must be admitted logically and in the last resort that all 'utilities and conveniences' are non-material; that is to say, they consist of the 'services' rendered by instruments. When thus tracked down, commodities will be found to be forms or modes of satisfaction produced or induced by instruments which may be material or immaterial. Now, if we were to regard these modes of satisfaction as the only commodities with which we could deal, we should find that no practical object could be gained by an attempt to analyse or give quantitative value to production. For we should have to acknowledge that these commodities must be estimated differently, according to the particular person to whose service they were applied, and depended as regards quantity in a large measure upon the passing physical or mental condition of the recipient. In fact, the foundation of political economy would be laid in those deep and dark recesses of psychology which can never be sufficiently explored to admit of exact quantitative measurements. If, then, we are not prepared to regard shelter, warmth, satisfaction of hunger, and the other countless modes of satisfaction or pleasure as the real commodities with which production is concerned, are we prepared to apply the term exclusively to the instruments which produce these modes of feeling? In that case a carriage will be a commodity, whether it belongs to a carriage-owner who lets it out on hire or to a private person who uses it exclusively for his own pleasure; a house will be a commodity, whether hired or owned by the occupier; a steamship will be a commodity, whether it belong to a great company and is used as part of their capital for conveyance of goods or passengers, or whether it be a private pleasure boat. Now, if we were to adopt this meaning, we should not attain the object which we sought by a term which should express the final result of the whole process of production as distinguished, on the one hand, from the machinery of production, and, on the other hand, from the intermediate stages through which a piece of wealth passed before it became a useful or pleasant object to a consumer. Thus, neglecting the accurate logical inquiry whether the object which renders a service or the service rendered has a better claim to be called a commodity, we propose to make the test one of possession, so as to include under commodity any material object or any service which has been bought for the exclusive use of the purchaser or of his friends to whom he may present it.

It is, of course, true that persons who buy houses or carriages for their own use change their minds and sell these commodities, or the unconsumed portion of them, or use them as a means of getting an income. So, too, certain commodities which are extremely durable, such as houses or even furniture, may be handed down from father to son, and the use of them or the consumption of a part of them regarded as part of the income of the temporary possessor. But it is convenient and even necessary not to go behind the immediate intentions of the purchaser of commodities, and to consider that he who purchases any commodity with the immediate desire to use it, demands, and from the point of view of economics, consumes the whole of the commodity.[1]

[1] The extent of the inaccuracy of economic treatment of commodities is well pointed out by Professor Sidgwick in his 'Principles of Pol. Econ.,' Book II., Ch. I.

Commodities will thus admit of the following classification:—

1. All material wealth in the possession of a consumer of which the consumption is an immediate utility or convenience, *e.g.*, food.
2. All material wealth in possession of a consumer of which the use (consumption being indirect or protracted) produces a utility or convenience, *e.g.*, houses, carriages, clothes, furniture, coal, &c.
3. All services rendered—(1) By another person, *e.g.*, the waiting of a servant, the advice of a physician; (2) By material wealth belonging to another, *e.g.*, conveyance in a train or hired carriage.

CHAPTER II.

THE BALANCE OF PRODUCTION AND CONSUMPTION.

SINCE the end and object of commerce is to produce those 'necessaries and conveniences' to which the term commodity is applied, it is useful to have some further term which shall include all these repositories of value, together with all those things which have contributed to form their value. Since everything which is a means[1] to the production of value itself possesses value, the term which is required will apply to all things possessing value. The word most suitable to express the sum of all values is wealth. This use of the word is wider than either the ordinary average meaning of the word, or the various meanings which economists have thought fit to attach to it. It includes not only all 'necessaries and conveniences,' material or immaterial, but all valuable things which

[1] The term 'means' is not intended to be synonymous with 'condition.' An atmosphere, and various other positive and negative conditions, material or non-material, may be essential to the production of commodities and they may possess no 'value.'

are on the way to become 'necessaries and conveniences,' and also all valuable things which assist these latter in their progress towards the goal of commodity.

Economists have been led into difficulties in defining wealth through their desire to keep as close as possible to the ordinary average meaning of the word. Since this ordinary meaning is approximately though not precisely confined to material objects of value, it has generally been thought best to exclude both services and abilities from wealth. This exclusion has caused much trouble in dealing with the use of capital and of labour, and especially in dealing with income. The exclusion is in fact quite illegitimate in any reasonable theory of economics. There are no doubt practical conveniences subserved by excluding them. They are incapable of exact measurement, and thus cannot be set off as value against a quantity of material goods. It makes political economy simpler to exclude all considerations save those of material values. But such simplicity is only attained by the sacrifice of logical method and practical usefulness alike. A political economy which takes account of the direct increase of material wealth brought about by the aggregation of masses of workers in large cities, but which takes no account of the effects of this change upon the physique and morale of the community, can have no claim to be a science capable of reaching truths which are of any practical importance to any State or any individual.

The illogicality of excluding human abilities is peculiarly patent. Though inseparable from the persons of their owners, their use is saleable. Labour-power must be regarded as an agent in production on the same footing with inanimate machinery; the two are constantly changing places as well as co-operating in production, and it is essential that they should be brought under some common term expressive of the element of productive value which they both possess.

In order to realise clearly the fuller meaning here assigned to wealth, we may adopt the following classification:—

I. All commodities, or things on the way to become commodities (*i.e.*, α. raw materials, β. unfinished goods, γ. finished goods, δ. commodities). These objects of commerce may be sub-divided into—

A. Material, *e.g.*, shoes in their finished or earlier stages of production.

B. Non-material, *e.g.*, a song or a professional opinion in its final or earlier stages of production.

II. The agents in production of commodities:

A. Material: consisting in,

(*a.*) Natural agents, including land, mines, &c.

(*b.*) Plant: buildings and machinery of commerce, either finally constructed, or in process of construction. Money as part of the machinery of exchange comes under this head.

B. Non-material: labour-power, comprising manual strength and skill, intelligence, honesty, &c., of those men engaged in the work of production, either of commodities or of the material machinery, or of those engaged in the furtherance of effective labour-power.

Keeping still in view the fact that the whole structure of commerce is designed to supply commodities to consumers, and returning to the division of the various phases in the production of commodities which we have already noticed, we shall obtain a clear idea of a certain necessary apportionment of the various forms of wealth in accordance with the work they are to do as agents or material of production. The commercial necessity which compels every commodity to pass through a number of earlier stages of existence in the gradual acquisition of its full value, requires also that at each stage there shall be situate a supply of machinery of production to assist it in its onward journey. Thus the whole organism of commercial life may be rightly represented in relation to the work of producing commodities, and will present the following picture :—

R. M.	(Natural Agents.—	Plant.--	Labour).
R. M.^{1}	"	"	"
R. M.^{2}	"	"	"
Goods	"	"	"
G.^{1}	"	"	"
G.^{2}	"	"	"
Shop G.	"	"	"
Com.	"	"	"

At each step in the process there will be a portion of the raw material on its way to become a commodity, a portion of natural agents in the shape of land, &c. (important in production of agricultural commodities, less important in other cases), a portion of plant in the shape of factories, storehouses, and machinery, and a portion of human labour.

In a well-organised industrial society it is evident

that these three agents in production (natural agents, plant, labour) will have a definite relation to the work they are to do at each stage in the process of production; that is to say, they will bear, both as a whole and singly, a definite proportion to the quantity of raw material in its various stages which it is their business to assist. Given the amount of R. M.[1] or R. M.[2] on its way to become commodities, a certain definite amount of each of the agents in production will be required to assist in furthering the work. An excess of all or any of these agents in production at any stage in the process is useless, and will not exist in a perfectly constructed commercial society, a deficiency of all or any of the same will impede the proper progress of some portion of raw material and will render useless a portion of agents at the further stages corresponding in amount to the deficiency. If, for example, to return to the process of producing shoes, there at any time existed more shoemaking machinery than was required for working into shoes the leather in stock, there would be a mere waste of so much machinery; if, on the other hand, there were a deficiency in the same machinery, not only would a certain amount of leather remain unmade into shoes, but a certain proportion of the capital of shoe merchants and retailers which was to have been occupied in bringing these shoes into the condition of commodities will be rendered useless. We are here, of course, assuming a stable condition of the manufacturing arts. If a new kind of shoemaking machine be discovered which costs no more to produce, but which will turn out twice as many shoes as the old machines, the amount of capital required at this stage in the production of shoes is half what it was before. But, assuming this stability in the arts of production, the amount of capital required at each stage bears an exact and fixed relation to the amount of consumption of commodities, and any excess or deficiency throws out of gear the whole machinery of production.

Excess or deficiency in natural agents or in labour at any point in the process will produce a similar result. In the actual world of commerce it is true that this exact relation between the agents in production and the raw material is seldom reached and never long maintained, but in so far as the actual state errs from this ideal there is a loss of economic energy.

The next step is to clearly recognise that there is a definite quantitative relation between the raw material at the different stages in production (the total amount of raw material, including under the term all goods short of commodity), and the total of commodities. If we were to assume that all raw material on its way to become commodities were obliged to pass through all those stages we have named, R. M., R. M.^{1}, &c., it is clear that in order to supply a definite quantity of commodities there must have been a certain definite and precise amount of R. M., which afterwards assumed the form R. M.^{1}, then R. M.^{2}, and so on right through the series. In that case a given total of commodities at any time would enable us to tell the exact quantity of R. M. which had previously existed at each of the successive stages in production. Any excess above this amount would have been useless for the proximate end production of commodities, any deficiency would have been impossible. But the simplicity of this calculation is marred by the fact that all commodities are not forced to pass through the same number of stages in production. Some pass straight from R. M. to goods, or have only one intermediate stage; many goods pass straight into shop-goods without passing through the stages G.[1], G.[2]. Hence a mere knowledge of the quantity of commodities produced would not enable one to tell the quantitative relation which had previously existed between the raw material at its different stages. To tell this accurately we should also have to know the character of the commodities produced, so as to clearly recognise through what stages each had passed. Possessing this knowledge of the quantity and nature of any given quantity of commodities, it would be theoretically possible to give an accurate description of the previous condition of the points R. M., R. M.[1], R. M.[2], &c., so far as the quantity of raw material situate at each of them were concerned. But we have previously admitted that a definite economic relation must exist between the quantity of raw material at each point and the quantity of agents in production. We now, therefore, reach this further step, that a given quantity of commodities of a known nature determines absolutely the amount of raw material, *plus* agents in production, previously existent at each stage in the process of production. But the raw material in its various states and the agents in production constitute the whole wealth of a community. Therefore a given quantity of commodities of a known nature determines the amount of wealth previously existent at each stage so far as the production of these commodities is concerned. It follows, then, that a knowledge of the total of commodities produced at any time in a country would enable us to tell the exact amount of wealth which had previously existed at each stage in the work of production. But if we know the amount of wealth at each stage we know the total amount of wealth. Therefore a knowledge of the total of commodities produced at any time will enable us to tell the total amount of wealth which has previously been engaged or used in the production of these commodities. Since the only use of wealth from the economic standpoint is to assist in producing commodities, the knowledge of the quantity of commodities produced in a community will enable us to tell the total amount of wealth which has had an economic[1] existence in the past. We may then state our conclusion thus:

There is a definite quantitative relation between the total amount of commodities produced in the present, and the total amount of wealth in various shapes which has usefully existed in the past. But the total amount of commodities produced in the present means, as we have seen, nothing else than the present rate of consumption, for a commodity is only finally produced when it is handed over to a consumer. We arrive then at the statement that

[1] By the term 'economic existence' as applied to wealth, we mean to cover such products as actually function as wealth, excluding any temporary surplus which could have at the time no economic use either for consumption or production. This surplus we consider later.

there exists at any time a fixed quantitative relation [1] between the present rate of consumption and the aggregate of wealth which has had an economic existence in the immediate past.

This is such an obvious truth that it may seem unnecessary to dwell upon it so emphatically. But it is, in fact, due chiefly to the neglect of this obvious truth that writers on economics have failed to construct a system which recommends itself with convincing force. We are, therefore, at the risk of being tedious, obliged to reiterate. The law of quantitative relation applies not only to the relation of the mass of consumption to the mass of wealth, but of the mass of consumption to the several parts of the process of production. If the raw material situate at any time at R. M. does not regularly advance to R. M.', and in due order pass through all the stages until it becomes commodities, it must accumulate somewhere, and such accumulation will tend to decay, or at any rate stand useless. For example, the stock of milk and eggs possessed by a dairyman at any given time must bear a definite due proportion to his sales of milk, eggs, &c. It is of no use for him to increase his stock of these articles if his sales do not increase. Similarly, the stock of

[1] It must be borne in mind, however, that this law of quantitative relation does not imply that the same quantity of commodities always requires the same quantity of wealth to assist in producing it. The changes in effectiveness of human or machine labour, owing to new inventions, greater manual skill, improved organisation of labour, &c., are continually altering the proportion of agents in production required to assist in producing a given quantity of commodities.

milch cows, hens, &c., kept by the farmer must bear a due proportion to his sales of milk, eggs, poultry, &c.; if his sales increase, so must his stock; if his sales decrease, so must his stock. What holds of one trade holds of all trades; the aggregate stock at each stage of production must bear a due relation to the sales effected. In a word, the quantity of wealth in existence and functioning as wealth cannot increase or diminish except in a constant relation with immediately future consumption.

It must be borne in mind, however, that the rate of consumption is not the only thing which limits the amount of wealth which can exist in the form of R. M. or goods or machinery. The number of available labourers or the amount of available natural agents may limit the amount of goods or machinery which can be used for production. It is true that the limit of natural agents is generally not absolute, but in accordance with the law of diminishing return to labour and capital employed in agriculture; but a particular manufacture might be absolutely limited by the amount of R. M. which could be procured. The limit of labourers is an absolute limit. Assuming that all available labourers are working with the utmost skill and energy the maximum quantity of the best machinery, the economic existence of any larger quantity of machinery or of more goods is clearly impossible. Under our definition of wealth we had included commodities, R. M. in its various stages, natural agents and plant, and lastly, labour-power.

Since, however, a quantitative relation must exist between consumption and wealth, it is evident that consumption and production must be similarly related. Every product must either be consumed or added to accumulated wealth, and the fact that a quantitative relation exists between consumption and wealth involves the existence of a more or less definite relation between consumption and production.

There are two alternative theories of the relation between production and consumption, each of which is theoretically possible. The first is that almost universally accepted by the best-known writers on political economy, viz., that production determines consumption under all circumstances, resting on the assumptions that whatever is so produced must be consumed, and that nothing can be consumed which has not been produced. The other possible theory is that consumption determines production in that the final cause or end of a process may be rightly said to determine the earlier steps in that process. Now, we state these two theories lest it should be thought that the law of quantitative relation between production and consumption depends for its validity upon one or other of them. In truth, it depends on neither, but is consistent with and required by both. We are not at present concerned with the discussion whether the amount consumed is determined or caused by the amount produced or the amount produced by the amount consumed, but merely assert that there must exist a quantitative relation between the two.

We have now to introduce the much-debated term, capital. It would be useless to attempt a full discussion of the various definitions of capital. In endeavouring to give a satisfactory meaning to the word two things are necessary. First, that the word shall cover certain definite kinds of wealth; second, that its meaning shall be kept as near as possible to the ordinary average meaning, for unless it is so kept it would be better even to invent some new collocation of letters rather than introduce a term which is bound to cause confusion. Most definitions of economists have proved futile because they have aimed at fulfilling too exactly the logical function of definition, and have embodied either a reference to the origin of capital or to the purpose for which it is to be used.

It has been described as 'the result of saving' by those who have not yet explained what 'saving' means, and who afterwards appear to include in savings the food which is not saved but consumed by labourers. It is also described as wealth which is 'destined' or 'devoted' to assist future production, so that 'the distinction between capital and not capital does not lie in the kind of commodities, but in the mind of the capitalist,'[1] and depends on his intention. If we are unable to say whether a particular piece of wealth which exists is or is not at the present time capital, it is absurd to maintain that our term capital can be a useful part of our economic nomenclature.

As our object is to give a definite meaning to the term which shall enable our readers to know exactly what things are and are not capital, we offer what is rather a description than a definition, and say that capital is that wealth which by its use directly assists production. But even this description is far too wide,

[1] Mill, 'Pol. Econ.,' Book I., Ch. IV., s. 1.

and it will presently be necessary to exclude certain kinds of wealth in order to trim our term to a closer accord with the ordinary meaning of the term. What are the kinds of wealth which, by their use, directly assist production? They would seem to include :—1. Plant and all machinery. 2. Raw material and goods in their various stages of development. 3. Labour-power (including skill, honesty, &c.) 4. Natural agents, land, mines, &c. 5. Commodities which, by their consumption, assist to produce labour-power. Now it is clear that if capital is to include all these forms, not only will it have passed far beyond the bounds of its ordinary use, but we shall require another term when we come to deal with the relations between the landowner, the employer of labour, and the labourer in regard to the sharing of the commodities they assist to produce. This broad meaning would include all wealth except luxuries in the hands of consumers; that is to say, those commodities which, by their consumption, do not minister either directly or indirectly to our productive energy, and which, since they cannot be entirely without effect, must be considered rather as impairing that energy, and deserving rather the appellation of 'illth' than that of wealth. The absurd attempt to include under capital the food and clothing of labourers, so far as it conduces to assist labour-power, sins both by making it impossible to say whether a particular piece of wealth is capital, and by militating against the common commercial meaning of the term.

Let us now turn to the different kinds of wealth which seem to fall under our description of capital, and by excluding what is necessary, restore the term to its most convenient economic use. Since both convenience of economic treatment and common usage exclude labour-power from capital, it is clear that it must be excluded. Since commodities consumed by producers only affect production indirectly, through their effect on labour-power, they must also be excluded. The case of land and other natural agents is rather different. It should be remarked that none of the economic definitions of capital have succeeded in excluding the value of land. For not only is land in large measure 'destined' to assist the production of wealth, but its value is, in fact, 'the result of past labour.' Not only does this last statement apply to the value put into land by landlords' or tenants' improvements, but also to the value created by the growth and activity of the community which forms what is now commonly known as the 'unearned increment.' Thus the whole value of land, alike that for which economic rent is paid and that which gets the average return of profit on capital invested, is the result of the work either of individuals or of the whole community, and may be said to be 'saved' or stored to assist future production. But while no definition can of right banish land value from capital, expediency may and does demand that it be treated separately, at least so far as that value not due to recent improvements is concerned. In so far as land and other natural agents stand distinct from the body of capital, and it is found convenient to treat them separately, in economic theory as in the actual calculations of commerce, we shall exclude them from our meaning of capital. We are now in a position to sum up the kinds of wealth which it is convenient to include under capital. They are, in fact, the first two of the five groups which fell under our former description, namely—(1) Raw material and goods in their various stages of development, including shop-goods; (2) plant and all machinery.

The distinction between what is capital and what is not capital, so far as the production of material forms of commodities is concerned, will be now quite clear; but, with regard to the production of non-material commodities, there occurs a difficulty for which no adequate solution can be found. Should the singing-lessons which assist in that voice-production which is to produce a commodity, songs, be regarded as labour or as non-material machinery? If the former, it is not capital; if the latter, it is. Or, again, is the work of examination-crammers to be regarded as a machine for producing passes, for these last are both commodities and instruments? The same difficulty applies to all that class of commodities commonly called services. So far as the efforts which produce them are concerned, the latter may be regarded either as labour or as non-material machinery. It would be more consistent with our theory to regard them as machinery, but common parlance would be inclined to describe them as forms of labour. Since, however, the theory of production and consumption is best illustrated from material forms of wealth, we may be content to leave it an open question whether the operations which produce services shall be classed as labour or as capital.

Having now assigned a clear meaning to the term

capital, we must bring the latter into relation with consumption. We have already seen that the different portions of this capital which function at the various stages in the process of production stand in a definite quantitative relation to the amount of immediately future consumption. We are therefore entitled to say that this future consumption limits the amount of capital which can economically exist in the present. If more capital should at any time exist than is required to assist in supplying future consumption, this excess is not real capital, as it cannot perform the true function of capital; it is merely nominal capital. That such excess of capital in any single trade may exist is, of course, readily acknowledged. The surplus may sometimes escape our notice from the fact that it does not necessarily stand quite idle. If in a certain factory there are twice as many machines as are required to do the work, either half of them may stand idle or all of them may be used for half-time or at half-pressure; in either case we should say that the real capital consisted in half the machines, the other half being surplus or nominal capital.

Now, whether this distinction is, in fact, applicable to commerce as a whole we are not yet in a position to assert. We can, however, say that, assuming it to be possible that the capital of a community at any time is more than is economically required to supply the commodities which that community consents to consume in the future, that excess will not be real but nominal capital. This distinction assumes a greater importance when it is applied to the fund from which capital is drawn, savings. If future consumption assigns a limit to real capital in the present, it must also assign a limit to real saving. Now, the idea of any possible limit to the present efficient thrift of a community imposed by the condition of future consumption is one which almost all economic writers have steadily refused to entertain. We must, however, maintain that, assuming it to be possible that some capital can exist in excess of what is required and be merely nominal capital, it would follow that the saving which provided that capital was not real but nominal saving.

What is saving? If a community consumes annually as much wealth as it produces, it obviously does not save. If it consumes less than it produces, the difference accumulates, and is called 'savings. 'Savings,' then, are the difference between what is produced and what is consumed. The correct formula is as follows, Production – consumption = savings. Since we can conceive production indefinitely increased and consumption maintained at a minimum, it is clear that this formula places no limit on savings. But just as real capital is capital for which there is a use, so real savings are savings for which there is a use, and, assuming that any portion of this difference between production and consumption goes to furnish merely nominal capital, it would obviously not find a use, and would be rightly distinguished as nominal saving.

Now, we are fully aware that almost all writers on economics will scoff at this distinction between real and nominal capital and saving as 'mere moonshine,' so firmly rooted is their conviction that whatever is produced will be consumed, and that there is no possible limit to the amount of capital that is wanted in a country. They utterly refuse to entertain the notion that any wealth which is 'saved' in the sense of being kept from immediate consumption can be useless for the purpose of assisting production. Thrift is the source of national wealth, and the more thrifty a nation is the more wealthy it becomes. Such is the common teaching of almost all economists; many of them assume a tone of ethical dignity as they preach the infinite value of thrift; this note alone in all their dreary song has caught the favour of the public ear. It is not, however, with the ethical value of saving that we are concerned, but with the economic doctrine of the possibility of infinite saving and the use of infinite capital.

To all who have followed our argument thus far, as, indeed, to all who have ever considered the function of capital, it should be clear that the capital of a community cannot be advantageously increased without a subsequent increase in consumption of commodities. A belief in the infinite possibility of saving implies, therefore, a belief in the infinite increase of consumption. In Chapter IV. we shall deal with the assertion that an increase in production forces a corresponding increase in consumption. But here we would call attention to the fact that there is a school of economic writers who have signally failed to recognise that every increase in saving and in capital requires, in order to be effectual, a corresponding increase in immediately future consumption. They will not admit that if people wish to save more now they must consent to spend more in the future. Since Mr. Mill, more than any other, is responsible for the popularity of this theory of the possibility of infinite saving and infinite capital, it will be worth while here to briefly examine his position.

Mr. Mill has two positions on the subject of saving. One is that saving may increase indefinitely without reference to increased consumption; the other, dependent on the former, consists in a contradiction of the assertion, 'production − consumption = saving,' by maintaining that "everything which is produced is consumed, both what is saved and what is said to be spent."[1] Now, by increase of saving, Mill only means one thing—addition to the wages-fund. If his capitalists refuse to consume their usual luxuries, the result of their abstinence, the savings, go to swell the wages-fund; either more labourers are employed, or the labourers already employed get higher wages. If there are no more labourers to employ, 'the whole of what was previously expended in luxuries, by capitalists and landlords, is distributed among the existing labourers in the form of additional wages. We will assume them to be already sufficiently supplied with necessaries. What follows? That the labourers become consumers of luxuries; and the capital previously employed in the production of luxuries is still able to employ itself in the same manner, the difference being that the luxuries are shared among the community generally, instead of being confined to a few.'[2] It is clear that this process is capable of indefinite expansion; the wages-fund is a bottomless fund into which any quantity of savings may be poured. If all savings (beyond what is required to

[1] Mill's 'Pol. Econ.,' Book I., Ch. V., s. 8 and s. 6.
[2] Book I., Ch. V., s. 3.

make such additions to plant and R. M. as increase in consumption may render desirable) goes into wages-fund, and for that reason ranks as economic saving and economic capital, it is clear that there is no limit assigned to saving and capital by any consideration of future consumption. If a mere addition to wages-fund is effectual saving, not only does future consumption place no limit on capital, but not even does production. An increase in the wages-fund, the result of which is to enable labourers to consume luxuries, obviously adds nothing to their producing power. Mill's theory, then, admits an indefinite expansion of capital, without any effect either on production or consumption. It is true he is not consistent in his language, but speaks in one passage of 'an increased production,' which apparently is to follow 'the increased accumulation,' and which 'might, rigorously speaking, continue, until every labourer had every indulgence of wealth consistent with continuing to produce.'[1] But why or how this increase of production should take place he does not explain. He does not assume, nor would he have any right to assume, a surplus of unemployed labour. How, then, can the increase of wages-fund have any result in increasing production? If it cannot increase production, what motive can induce capitalists to save? The only conceivable motive at work could be a desire to present to their labourers the luxuries which they refused to consume themselves. And this act of amiable and foolish philanthropy is what Mill means by 'saving.' His process of reasoning is apparently

[1] Book I., Ch. V., s. 3.

this: the wages-fund, however large or small, is always productively employed, for it is used to assist labour to produce wealth; by abstaining from my usual luxuries I can increase the wages-fund; therefore I can add to the productive employment of wealth. It is evident that Mill's 'savings,' which go to increase the luxuries of the working man, are not real or economic savings.

To ascertain the exact point at which Mill's argument is vitiated by error, it is only necessary to test his extreme hypothesis (quoted above) by assuming that a farming landowner gains as rent and profit from his land £.1,100 a-year, and that he pays away to twenty labourers £.1,000 a-year (£.50 a-year each). The gross income derived from the land is thus £.2,100 a-year, and the whole of this sum is distributed to all concerned and consumed. Subsequent to the supposed abstinence, the farming landowner, instead of taking £.1,100 for himself and paying his labourers £.50 a-year each, distributes the gross income of the farm, £.2,100, amongst the twenty-one individuals concerned (the twenty labourers and himself) equally, each receiving £.100 a-year. It is evident that, under these circumstances, Mill is quite right in asserting that there is no decrease in consumption. The labourers consume just as much more as the landowner consumes less, or, as Mill puts it, 'luxuries are shared among the community generally instead of being confined to a few.' But it is evident that Mill is wrong when he infers, as his argument requires, that the landowner is saving £.1,000 a year (the sum by which he has reduced his personal expenditure). The gross income derived from the farm is £.2,100 a-year, and the whole of this sum is expended as absolutely and completely in the one case as the other, and it is quite evident that the landowner saves nothing by his abstinence. If, as Mill's argument requires, he saves £.1,000 a-year, then the aggregate consumption must be reduced to £.1,100 a-year; but if this is the case, the labourers' wages are not raised, and they derive no direct benefit from the landowners' saving operations. Mill, therefore, is incorrect when he states that in this hypothesis the 'rich' lay by, from conscientious motives, the surplus of their profits: the rich do nothing of the sort; they cease to expend their incomes themselves and hand over these unexpended incomes as a free gift to their labourers, but they effect no saving of any sort, and nothing is 'laid by.' The hypothesis, therefore, fails absolutely to answer the problem with which Mill is dealing, whether, 'if consumers were to save and convert into capital more than a limited portion of their income, and were not to devote to unproductive consumption an amount of means bearing a certain ratio to the capital of the country, the extra accumulation would be merely so much waste.' All that the hypothesis proves is, that if some individuals cease to spend the whole of their incomes themselves, and give away the surplus portions to others who do expend them, then no undue accumulations will result, a conclusion with which we entirely agree.

Mill, in fact, does not merely ignore the consideration of how his increased capital is represented in an increase of production and consumption, but he further contradicts the self-evident proposition, 'production – consumption = saving,' by maintaining the tenet that 'what is saved is consumed equally with what is spent.' His words are these: 'Everything which is produced is consumed; both what is saved and what is said to be spent, and the former quite as rapidly as the latter.'[1] 'The word saving does not imply that what is saved is not consumed, nor even necessarily that its consumption is deferred; but only that if consumed immediately it is not consumed by the person who saves it.'[2] It might at first appear that when Mr. Mill maintained that savings were consumed, he meant those savings accumulated in the shape of plant, machinery, &c., the material forms of which are gradually destroyed in the use made of them; 'consumed,' in this sense, would be synonymous with 'used.' But when he adds that 'what is saved' is consumed 'quite as rapidly as what is spent,' it is clear that he is thinking only of those savings which go to swell the wages-fund. Now, in what sense can these be said to be saved? Mr. Mill would reply that they are saved in the sense that they form a part of capital and are productively consumed. That which goes into the wages-fund is, *ipso facto*, 'productively consumed.' The capitalists abstain from consuming luxuries, thereby increasing the wages-fund, so that the labourers consume the luxuries which the capitalists denied themselves. This consumption of luxuries by the labourers is to be productive consumption, though the consumption of the same articles by the capitalists is unproductive consumption. The only difference is, that the same luxuries are in the one case consumed by one class

[1] Book I., Ch. V., s. 6. [2] I., V., s. 5.

of people; in the other case, by another class. The formal act of having formed a part of a wage-fund entitles these articles to rank as wealth which has been productively consumed. In what sense were they productively consumed? True, they are consumed by a class of 'producers,' but we must not forget that the capitalist is also a producer. They are not any more than before consumed in such a way as to assist production. Mr. Mill has shown no way in which an indefinite increase of his wages-fund increases production; he has not made good his contention that 'every increase of capital gives, or is capable of giving, additional employment to industry.'[1] The same wealth is used in the same way by two different classes of people; in the one case it is said to be spent, in the other to be

[1] I., V., s. 3. Prof. Fawcett, though he follows Mill, as usual, in reckoning as capital everything which has formed part of a wages-fund, admits that there is a difference between this nominal capital and real capital; in fact, that there is capital which cannot function as capital. 'It has been shown in this chapter that the capital which at any time exists in a country is always sufficient to administer to the production of a much greater amount of wealth than that which is produced; in other words, the production of wealth which actually takes place might be effected with the aid of much less capital than the amount which is applied'——'For instance, every shilling of the labourers' wages which is expended upon anything but the mere necessaries of life might be destroyed without affecting the industrial efficiency of the labourer, and consequently without diminishing the future production of wealth' ('Pol. Econ.,' Book I., Ch. IV.). But Mr. Fawcett does not explain why he speaks of this portion of the wages as capital at all: it is not covered by his definition of capital as 'the wealth which is not immediately consumed unproductively, and which may, consequently, be devoted to assist the future production of wealth' (p. 19). There is no possible way open whereby this portion of the labourers' wages can assist the future production of wealth.

saved. It is clear that if wealth be added to the wages-fund which cannot be productively used, it cannot be rightly said to be saved. It is consumed just as soon, in the same manner and with no different results, whether it be labourers' luxuries or capitalists' luxuries. It is, in fact, neither saved nor productively consumed. What motive can have induced capitalists to thus increase the wages-fund without increasing the amount of production or the sum of gross profits for themselves, it is impossible to imagine. Mr. Mill himself acknowledges that " when these classes turn their income into capital they do not thereby annihilate their power of consumption; they do but transfer it from themselves to the labourers, to whom they give employment." But he does not seem to recognise that by thus increasing the wages-fund they give no more employment; that, in fact, the wealth they hand over is consumed just as unproductively as before, and is in no sense saved.

Of course throughout this argument we have accepted Mill's supposition, that there is no new or unemployed class of labourer whose work and wants are to be considered. But even in the statement of this alternative case Mill's argument is confused and incorrect. His words are as follows:—'Either there is or is not an increase of their numbers (*i.e.*, of labourers) proportional to the increase of capital. If there is, the case presents no difficulty. The production of necessaries for the new population takes the place of the production of luxuries for a proportion of the old, and supplies exactly the amount of employment which has been lost.' Now, in the first place, this idea, that before a new population can be set to work at all a separate stock of necessaries has to be got together and added to the previous wages-fund, will be seen to be totally erroneous. In the second place, assume that this stock of necessaries were added to the wages-fund and used to employ the new labourers, the difficulty is only got over for the moment. A new difficulty arises. What about the wealth produced by the new labourers? How is it to be consumed? The new labourers have already got a stock of necessaries provided for them in the new wages-fund, constantly maintained by a continuance of the former abstinence of the capitalists. The wealth, then, which the new labourers produce must either go to provide luxuries for themselves or for the old class of labourers, or it must provide luxuries for the capitalists, who will thus be obliged to revoke their vow of abstinence. To one or two or all of these uses it must be put, and in any case it will be unproductively consumed in the shape of luxuries.

It follows, then, alike from the *à priori* principle embodied in the law of quantitative relation and from consideration of its application in the cases adduced by Mr. Mill, that an indefinite increase of effective saving and of capital is impossible, unless a corresponding increase in immediately future consumption takes place.

It is easy to understand how Mill, and those who held with him the theory of a special wages-fund, could see no necessity for assigning a limit to the amount of effectual saving which a community might accomplish. This wages-fund was a bottomless vessel into which you might go on pouring any amount of saving without any chance of an overflow or surplus. If the class of saving individuals were content to abstain from consuming, and to hand over continually to productive labourers their command over commodities without seeking anything in return, there is no reason why they should not do so, and call it 'saving,' if they prefer the term. But most modern economists have rejected this theory, recognising that no motive was provided which could invite saving individuals to increase indefinitely this wages-fund, since labourers would not thereby become more productive, and if they did the saving individuals would not be willing to consume the increase of products. But, strange to say, those who have most distinctly repudiated the wage-fund theory have retained the theory of the possibility of infinite saving which depended on it. We still hear from economists constant commendation of indiscriminate thrift; with a steady fall of profit before their face they do not recognise the possibility of an excess of saving; that however much is saved all can find a full economic use in assisting further production, is accepted as an axiom of their economics. The following sentences of Mill still represent the accepted theory of saving: "The fund from which saving can be made is the surplus of the produce of labour after supplying the necessaries of life to all concerned in the production; as much as this, though it never is saved, always might be." "The amount of this fund, this net produce, this excess of production over the physical necessaries of the producers, is one of the elements that determine the amount of saving. The greater the produce of labour after supporting the labourers, the more there is which can be saved." [1] Now, we would ask our readers to put the question clearly to themselves. Could a community save all it could produce with the exception of necessaries of life? If saving be taken merely to mean 'not consuming,' it is obvious that this is possible. But saving means something more than this. It signifies not only abstention from consumption, but application as a means of further production. If the whole of this surplus can be saved, it must be necessary then to show that it can be used to produce other things which are wanted. If it is not used to assist in producing other things, or if the other things are not wanted, the saving is in vain, or rather, it is not saving but mere waste.

Turning to the sentence quoted from Mill, let us suppose the total produce of a community to be represented by one hundred, and that out of this forty sufficed to supply 'the necessaries of life to all concerned in the production,' and that the other sixty were hitherto consumed as luxuries, would it be possible, instead of consuming these sixty as luxuries, to save them and apply them in assisting further production? To the question thus put the answer is plain. Not merely is there already sufficient capital to aid production of 'the necessaries of all concerned in the production,' but capital previously applied to produce the luxuries; the result would be that not merely is there no use for the new increment of capital, but of that previously existing the portion hitherto devoted to the production of luxuries can no longer be used. Con-

[1] Mill, 'Prin. Pol. Econ.,' Book I., Ch. XI., s. 1.

sumption being reduced from one hundred to forty, it is obvious that either production must be reduced in like proportion, in which case the aggregate of capital required will be similarly reduced, or articles will be produced for which there is no use present or prospective.

Again, let us look at the effects, in a more concrete form, of a general endeavour to save the whole of the surplus of the produce of labour. Consumption, which previously included (1), the necessaries of productive labourers; (2), the necessaries of others than productive labourers; (3), all luxuries; would now be confined to the first of these three classes. It is evident, in the first place, that all the portion of the stock of the community which previously served to satisfy the desire for luxuries can no longer be so applied, and since there is no other use for it present or prospective, this stock must be absolutely valueless, and the fortunes or savings of individuals which existed in these forms of capital must be extinguished. Thus, for example, let it be assumed that every form of potable alcohol is included in the term 'luxury,' the existing stocks of wine, beer, and spirits will now be absolutely without value, and the fortunes, savings, &c., which they represent will be destroyed. Similarly, all other materials of luxury will become as worthless as alcohol to a community of rigid teetotallers. The value of a commodity depends upon the present or prospective existence of a consumer, who will be able to give an equivalent for it. So, if all consumption of luxuries ceased, the value of all existing materials of luxury is destroyed.

As to the second class, comprising the necessaries

of others than productive labourers, this will be equally void of value under the new condition. For those necessaries cannot be applied to increase the stock of necessaries of productive labourers, for this stock is already sufficient, and any increase would be either in the form of waste or luxury.

Since the only commodities to be consumed or enjoyed are the necessaries of productive labourers, there could be no object in producing anything but these necessaries. Now, the plant already in existence sufficed to replace the current consumption of all necessaries of producers and non-producers and all luxuries. All that portion of this plant not devoted to aiding the production of necessaries for producers is now rendered absolutely valueless, and the fortunes and savings represented therein are destroyed.

It will thus seem obvious that if the community limits its consumption to the necessaries of productive labourers, the only stock which can be of use is a stock of these necessaries, and the only plant which can be of use is the plant required to replace the necessaries consumed. The accumulated wealth per head of the population will thus be reduced to the lowest sum compatible with its continued existence. If we assume that in such a community as England one-half of the consumption consists of luxuries, the reduction in accumulated wealth per head thus brought about would be one-half, and, until the consumption per head of the community again increased, could not exceed that amount. The whole of the argument contained in this contention is so brief and so simple, it ought to require to be stated only once to find ready acceptance. If the community ceased to wear clothes, and limited its consumption to bread and cheese, what stock or what plant could be required or could possess exchange value other than that required to replace the current withdrawals of bread and cheese?

Neither Mill nor the English economists since Mill, who have dealt with the increase of capital, have pointed out how any increase in economic capital is thus absolutely limited by the condition of future consumption of commodities. And when we say future consumption, we do not refer to a future of ten, twenty, or fifty years hence, but to a future that is but little removed from the present. If we consider that part of capital which is devoted to retailing, it is evident that so soon as the stock of shop goods exceeds the quantity required to enable consumers to purchase the exact articles they require, with the maximum convenience to all concerned, the excess is over-supply. For instance, if x shop goods are sufficient to enable the current consumption to be supplied, any stock in excess of this total would be over-supply. If the stock of shop goods increases, a corresponding increase in consumption must at once take place, or the stock of shop goods will exceed the total that is economically desirable and over-supply will exist. When we follow back the processes of production, it is true a larger time element intervenes, but even here it must not be forgotten that the habits of the community are more or less regular and settled. If saving is being effected, not merely during one day or one week, but regularly and habitually, the constantly increasing total of capital thus brought about will require a regular and habitual increase in the rate of consumption to prevent over-supply in the earlier stages of production.[1] In addition to the limit imposed by the rate of consumption there is further the limit imposed by the other two requisites of production ; so soon as every labourer is provided with the plant and raw material requisite to his most efficient labour, or so soon as all the plant, &c., is provided requisite to the most efficient application of all the natural agents available, it is evident that no further accumulations of capital can be used, and must, if accumulated, remain idle and exist as over-supply.

If increased thrift or caution induces people to save more in the present, they must consent to consume more in the future. If they refuse to assent to this condition, they may persist in heaping up new material forms of capital, but the real effective capital will be absolutely limited by the actual extent of their future consumption. It is necessary to strenuously insist on this conclusion, since the want of a clear recognition of it prevents not only business men, but students of economics, from a proper understanding of the machinery of commerce. Our distinction between real and nominal capital is, then, as follows :—The nominal capital is a mere body, the real capital the same body so far as it is animated by productive force in economical work ; the same amount of this productive force may occupy a larger or a smaller number of material forms. If the future consump-

[1] Maintaining the existing stock of plant in repair and replacing it with new when worn out is not saving, it is merely keeping the existing total of capital intact. No individual or community can be said to save unless it increases its aggregate total of capital.

tion which limits the amount of real capital which can exist in the present be x., we shall have at each of the stages in the process of production, viz., R. M., R. M. ^{1}, R. M. ^{2}, &c., a certain definite amount of capital, both in the form of material of production and of machinery. This we will denote by y. The following, then, will denote the actual economic condition of commerce at any given time :—

R.M.	R.M.^{1}	R.M.^{2}	Goods.	G.^{1}	Shop Goods.	Commod.
y.	y.	y.	y.	y.	y.	x.

Now, while x. represents a definite quantity of forms of commodity for consumption, the number of material forms which constitute y. at any point may be greater or smaller in accordance with the strictness of economy which marks the process of production. The supply of x. commodities only requires that a certain number of forms of material should be transformed from R. M. to R. M.^{1}, and from R. M.^{1} to R. M.^{2}, and so on, and only requires the working of the smallest amount of machinery which suffices to perform this work. But at any of these points there may be found more than this requisite quantity of material forms or machines. In this case there is not more real capital than there would otherwise have been, but the same amount of real capital is distributed over a larger number of forms, the same quantity of producing power animates more faintly a larger number of producing bodies. Of course, if, owing to such excess of forms, any number of these forms stood absolutely idle, they could, hardly, be recognised to have any claim to be called capital. But it is possible that there should be an excess of forms of material or machine capital at any point, and that none of this should stand absolutely, or in any degree, idle. To return to our old example of the production of shoes, it is possible that there may be twice as much hides and twice as much machinery engaging in tanning as is required for the production of leather commodities for future consumption. It is not even necessary to suppose that the whole of the machinery does not work at full force. Double the amount of work and double the amount of production may go on at this point, but the amount of real capital employed there, from the point of view of the production and consumption of the community, is just the same as if half the work had been done with half the hides and half the tanning machinery. We are not saying that the capital is the same from the point of view of the individual tanner, or of the whole body of tanners. We shall presently see that capital and saving is, or may be, entirely different, as we look at them from the individual point of view and that of the community. Here we are only concerned with the production and consumption of the entire community. The production and consumption of the community only requires that a certain definite amount of tanning work should be done, and the real tanning capital from its point of view is the smallest amount of hides and machines requisite to do this amount of tanning. Assuming that more than this requisite amount of the forms of capital exists, it is nominal capital in excess of what the community requires; it is, in a word, over-supply. That such over-supply or excess of capital might exist at any one stage, or indeed in all the stages, in the production of one or more commodities, is generally conceded, but that it can exist in every line of production at the same time, assuming the form of a general over-supply, is pronounced impossible. But our law of quantitative relation between production and future consumption imposes no such qualification. As we deduced from it the possibility of over-supply in one branch of production, we can deduce with equal logical precision the possibility of a simultaneous over-supply at every point, that is, of general over-supply. Just as y. may at any one point in the productive process be embodied in a larger number of material forms of capital than is economically required, so it may be embodied at all points. We are, then, here entitled to affirm the theoretic possibility of general over-supply.

If there should exist at any time a larger number of forms of capital at any point or points in the process of production than is economically required for the current rate of consumption, this excess will figure as over-supply. But suppose that every increase in production, or every temporary or slight excess in these forms of capital, has power to force a corresponding increase of consumption, it is clear that this general over-supply can only exist as such for a merely nominal length of time, and that, when it has produced its effect by increasing consumption, it will figure as real capital with a full economic use.

In the next chapter we shall examine the actual phenomena of trade, and, instead of replying to this question by purely theoretic reasoning, we shall base our answer on admitted commercial facts.

In this chapter it has been shown that an exact quantitative relation must exist between the amount of useful capital and the rate of consumption. In Chapter IV. it will be shown that, in any period of depression in trade, the rate of consumption actually determines the amount of useful capital, and that, in such periods, only by first increasing the demand for commodities is it possible to increase the amount of real capital in the community.

CHAPTER III.

THE PHYSIOLOGY OF PRODUCTION.

FEW terms have caused more trouble in economics than supply and demand. It is necessary, there ore, to clearly emphasise the meanings which are given to them in this book. Taken in relation to an act of sale, they bear a different meaning according as they are regarded from the point of view of an individual or group of individuals and from that of the whole community. From the point of view of the individual member of a commercial community, every sale of any kind of goods is a quantity supplied and every purchase a quantity demanded. Thus, if a farmer goes to market with a quantity of wheat and sells it to a merchant, so far as the farmer is concerned the wheat has been demanded. If, however, the merchant still offers this same wheat for sale at the same market, it is evident that the quantity of wheat offered at the market has not been affected. The same aggregate of wheat is still offered, the only difference being that the ownership of a part of it has been transferred from the farmer to the merchant.

If, however, a miller purchases this wheat, it is withdrawn from the market, and no longer forms a part of the stock there offered; it has, so far as the market is concerned, been demanded and supplied. But when the community is considered as a whole, it is evident that this wheat is still offered for sale by the miller in the form of flour; in its new shape, with added value, it still constitutes a part of the general stock, and has not, so far as the community is concerned, been demanded and supplied. The community includes the farmer, the merchant, the miller, and the baker; and if the wheat is a part of the general stock when in the hands of the farmer, it must equally be so when in the hands of the merchant, the miller, or the baker. So soon, however, as the bread is bought by a consumer and consumed, the aggregate stock is affected; it is reduced by the exact total of such a purchase. The stock possessed by the community is decreased, so that as regards the whole community the wheat, in its final form of bread, has been demanded.

If, therefore, by the 'quantity demanded' be meant the quantity withdrawn from the general stock, demand can only mean that demand exercised by consumers, and does not include the inter-purchases and sales effected by the various classes of producers. It is necessary to insist upon this strict distinction. Wheat is habitually sold by one dealer to another, and passes through the hands of the miller and the baker before it is consumed in the form of loaves. If it were to count as supply on each occasion of its sale, and were said to be supplied and demanded each time, each bushel would reckon as a supply of as many bushels as the number of times it had been sold. The aggregate supply of wheat could thus be indefinitely increased by interposing additional 'middlemen' between the farmer and the baker, a conclusion which is absurd.

Thus, while from the point of view of an individual, or a class of individuals, the quantity of wealth bought or sold by such individuals or classes of individuals may be considered to be supplied and demanded, from the point of view of the community only those commodities which are bought by consumers can be said to be supplied or demanded. Since political economy is concerned primarily with the interests, not of private individuals, but of the whole community, the definition of such terms as supply and demand when used without qualification must evidently be made to accord with the larger point of view. Supply can now be defined without ambiguity as 'the aggregate of all goods (shop-goods) available for sale to consumers.' Demand is an ambiguous term, and it will be well to define separately 'quantity demanded' and 'demand,' in order that the latter may have only one meaning. 'Quantity demanded' is 'the aggregate of all shop-goods[1] bought by consumers.' 'Demand'[2] is 'the quantity of purchasing power' applied to purchase the 'quantity demanded.'

[1] Since, when shop-goods have been bought they are commodities, it would be more accurate to use the term commodity here, but to do so would introduce a possible misunderstanding as regards the relations of 'supply' and 'quantity demanded.'

[2] 'Demand' is more than ambiguous as a term in political economy. It seems to be used in at least four senses :—

1. As the equivalent of 'quantity demanded.'

But while political economy deals primarily with the production and consumption of wealth by the whole community, it is also necessary to examine the relation in which individuals and groups of individuals stand to one another; that is to say, to treat wealth from the point of view of narrower interests than that of the whole community. The addition to or abstraction from the wealth of an individual is, from his point of view, analogous to the addition to or abstraction from the total wealth of the community. We shall, therefore, be justified in using the convenient terms, 'supply' and 'demand,' in speaking of the purchases made from other producers than retail shopkeepers. So we shall speak of the supply of wheat and the demand for wheat, as well as the supply of loaves and the demand for loaves, although the exercise of a demand for wheat by the miller does not diminish the stock of wealth of the community, while a corresponding exercise of demand for loaves by the consumer does this. If there existed other convenient terms by which the two acts of purchase might be rightly distinguished, it would doubtless be less embarrassing; but since there are no other terms to describe the stock of incomplete commodities and the amount of purchasing power which is used to purchase them than supply and demand, we are compelled to apply these terms.

2. As purchasing power in general, whether actually applied to purchase shop-goods or not.
3. Purchasing power applied to purchase shop-goods (the definition here accepted).
4. The desire to obtain various forms of wealth, a conception which removes it out of all possible relation with supply as a quantity offered.

It must, however, be understood that when the terms are used without previous qualification they apply to the purchase of shop-goods or finished products.

It has already been seen that the only act of purchase or exercise of purchasing power which diminishes the stock of wealth of the community is the demand for shop-goods or finished products. Now, what is this purchasing power? The most convenient form of purchasing power is, of course, money; but every form of wealth contains a specialised form of this power, which can be exchanged for the general form of money. To the maker and the trader goods, raw material, plant, &c., are valued exclusively for the more or less of this purchasing power which they afford their owners. The owner is indifferent whether this purchasing power is embodied in the shape of otto of roses or guano, a steam-engine or a travelling pancrama; the one point he considers is the market value, the purchasing power which such possessions give. From the point of view of the individual tradesman, all acts of sale and purchase are primarily exchanges of forms of this purchasing power. When a baker sells bread for money he exchanges purchasing power in the shape of bread for purchasing power in the shape of money, and when he buys flour from the miller he exchanges purchasing power in the shape of money for purchasing power in the shape of flour. The baker considers himself equally rich; indeed, considers himself to possess just as much 'money,' whether he possesses one thousand sovereigns or a stock of flour which, at current prices, is worth £. 1,000. Again, from the point of view of the whole community, it will be evident that the aggregate amount of purchasing power possessed by the community is in no wise affected by sales and purchases of unfinished goods, of raw material, or of plant. In such acts of trade each individual retains a constant amount of purchasing power, and merely changes the shape in which he holds it.

So soon, however, as the consumer buys shop-goods or finished products the case is different. In this act a quantity of purchasing power is annihilated and ceases to exist. Take the case of the man who purchases a loaf for his consumption, paying 6 *d*. to the baker. It is true the baker has merely exchanged one form of purchasing power, a loaf, for another form, 6 *d*., but the consumer, who previously had 6 *d*., has now nothing, for that which he got in exchange he has consumed. Thus, we have identified the act of demand for a commodity with the extinction of purchasing power and the consumption of a portion of the total stock of wealth of the community.

The next step is to establish clearly the following propositions:—Firstly, that an exercise of demand (for commodities) cannot diminish capital; secondly, that an exercise of demand, though it consumes a portion of previously existent wealth and annihilates a portion of purchasing power, causes the production of an equivalent amount of new forms of wealth and purchasing power.

From what has been already said respecting purchasing power it will be evident that the capital of an individual shopkeeper cannot be diminished by the purchases of his customers at current prices. For every loaf a baker sells he receives money sufficient to buy flour and make another loaf, together with an element of profit which is not yet within our scope of inquiry. Whether the baker does or does not apply this money to replace the loaf he has sold, it cannot be said that his capital is diminished by the act of purchase. For capital is always reckoned in money values without consideration as to what quantity of it at any given time exists in the form of money, goods, or plant. Let us assume that it is a grocer with £.2,000 of grocery stores; this £.2,000 forms his capital, which he rigorously refuses to spend or consume. In three months' time every form in which this capital existed, every ounce of sugar, pound of tea, or side of bacon, will have been consumed, and may not even have been replaced in similar proportions of quantity; but in some shape or other, in new forms of goods, or in money in the till or at his bankers, this £.2,000 of capital will continue to exist. This is the meaning of commercial capital, in using which all merchants, statisticians, and political economists are in complete accord. So far as the capital of individuals is concerned, we shall not, therefore, ask for any other test than that of money estimate. From the individual's point of view it is the money value which he applies to the acquisition of an income. Since, then, the purchase of shop-goods by a consumer at current prices does not diminish the capital of the retailer, so the purchases of a retailer from a wholesale merchant, or of the latter from a manufacturer, do not diminish for a moment the capital which belongs to each respectively. Thus, it will appear that the normal rate of demand can have no effect in diminishing the stock of capital at any point in the organisation of industry. It has already been shown in the last chapter that no more capital can economically exist at any point in the productive process than is required to furnish commodities for the current rate of consumption. Hence, it is clear that a normal demand for commodities keeps in continuous existence the same amount of capital.

It now remains to establish the second point, that a normal exercise of demand causes the production of an amount of new forms of wealth equivalent to those consumed; that is to say, not only does capital enjoy a continuous existence, but the number of forms of each kind of capital exist continuously. It is clear that every individual form of capital perishes: if it is raw material or goods, it passes into the form of commodity, and is thus consumed; if it is plant or machinery, it is worn out by use or superseded by newer and more efficient forms. Is there any economic force which induces the production of fresh forms of capital to take the place of those which perish?

When shop-goods are purchased by a consumer, the price paid for them under normal conditions of trade is sufficient to enable the shopkeeper to replace the articles sold, and to yield him a margin of gain. This 'margin of gain,' or 'retailer's profit,' as it is sometimes loosely called, represents the whole difference between the wholesale and the retail price. It furnishes a fund out of which is paid the profit of the shopkeeper upon the capital in his business, his own wages, the wages of his *employés*, and the rent of his shop, &c. This 'margin of gain' provides, in fact, the income received by all those who assist production in the retail stage. But at this point in our argument it is only necessary to recognise that out of this margin of gain comes the element of personal gain or profit which is the inducement to the shopkeeper to ply his trade. The price received by the shopkeeper is sufficient, then, to enable him to replace the article he has sold and to retain a margin of gain.

But is there any influence at work which compels him to spend the money in replacing the article he has sold rather than retain the purchasing power in its shape of money or apply it to buy commodities for his own consumption? Yes, he is a tradesman, and as such seeks an income which is made of the profit on his sales, and in no other way. Thus, it is his interest to maintain his stock of shop-goods intact, so as to provide for expected sales. His capital is just as great if, instead of using the money he has received to purchase a similar article to that which he has sold, he keeps the money in his till, but his capital is not in the most advantageous form for the conduct of his trade and the getting of future profit. Hence, the shopkeeper is impelled by a force which is not the less natural and insuperable because it acts through the operation of his will, to continually replace the goods he sells to consumers by applying the price he receives (minus the margin of gain) as a demand for like goods from the store of the wholesale trader. The wholesale trader is impelled by the same force to replenish his diminished store by using the money he receives from the shopkeeper (again, minus his margin of gain) in purchasing a like quantity of articles from the manufacturer. And so the impulse passes along the whole line of production, compelling each producer to replace the form of goods which he has passed on to a further stage in production by using the money he has received for it to replace it by a similar form of goods. It will presently appear that he is compelled out of reasonable consideration for his own interest not only to keep the same number of forms of goods to meet the expected continuance of the present rate of sales, but also to replace every form of plant or machinery which is worn out in the course of production. To make this position clear let us take the production of some one commodity, say pianos. If we suppose the quantity of pianos demanded to be a regular one, we shall be justified in concluding that at any given time there will be a number of pianos in more and less finished states from the condition of raw material (wood, iron, &c.) to the condition of finished shop-goods, and that there will be a fixed relation between the amount of these piano-goods at the various stages of development. Now, if I go into a piano-shop and purchase a piano, the shopkeeper, seeking the profit which comes by selling pianos, will use the money I pay him to obtain another piano from the wholesale merchant so as to maintain his full stock; the merchant will use the money he receives to purchase another piano from the manufacturer, and so on. Thus, the money I pay the shopkeeper for a piano will be handed down along the whole line of production, each recipient abstracting a portion which shall serve as profit to himself, as wages to his labourers,[1] as a fund to repair the wear-and-tear of machinery and plant, and as rent for natural agents whose use he enjoys. The effect of this transmission of money along the whole line will be to move a portion of piano-material at each stage one further step, so as to fill the vacancy occasioned by my demand.

Since, further, my demand forms merely a portion of the ordinary current demand, it will have been expected and provided for all along the line. Thus, the shopkeeper, anticipating that he will on that day sell a piano, has ordered from the merchant a new piano to replace it. The merchant, anticipating this and other shopkeepers' orders, has ordered new pianos to replace them from the maker, and the maker, anticipating these orders, has engaged labour and provided the raw material requisite to execute them. Every individual engaged in the trade expects to sell every day a certain quantity of goods, and makes the necessary arrangements for supplying them. If the shopkeeper sells three pianos daily, on the average, he will order from the merchant three pianos daily, or say eighteen pianos a-week, and similarly with the merchant and manufacturer, so that each of these successive purchases do not reduce the stock of any of the traders in the line, but merely cause a general advance of piano-material, a shop-

[1] The term 'labourer' is used here to cover all those producers who receive wages from capitalists.

goods piano passing into commodity, and new raw material being created, thus :—

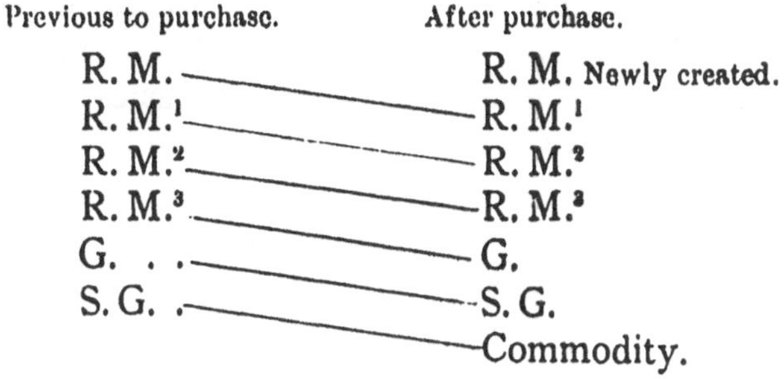

Thus the condition of piano material after my purchase will be precisely the same as before my purchase. Thus a continuity in the forms of piano goods is secured automatically by the natural result of an act of purchase of a shop good. Since the moving on of piano material at the various stages in production requires and employs a certain amount of forms of machinery and labour, in so far as this work of movement wears out the forms of machinery, it must set in operation a force which shall bring about the constant replenishment of these forms if the continuous demand for pianos is to be satisfied. As we saw that the piano seller was impelled by his own interest to employ the bulk of the price paid for a piano in purchasing another piano from the wholesale merchant, by the same consideration he is compelled to use another fraction of the price in maintaining his shop and premises in good repair, in advertising, and in otherwise maintaining his business in proper condition. So, also, the merchant is compelled to use a portion of the price he receives in keeping his warehouses in good repair. In the case of traders, this element of price which is spent in repairs of plant and machinery is often slight, but when we come to the makers it is more important. In order to get his usual rate of profit by maintaining his rate of sales, the maker must keep his machinery in good repair, and just as his interest impels him to replace goods he has sold, so it impels him to use a portion of the price he receives to repair machinery worn out in use. Thus a part of the price which comes to the piano manufacturer out of the price I paid for my piano must go to the makers or traders of new machinery, which is constantly required to replace worn-out machinery. As we conceived that there were pianos in every stage of development, so we must conceive that the machinery required in making pianos exists in every stage of development. So that as my purchase of a piano preserved the continuity of the forms of capital consisting of piano material in its various stages, so it will preserve the continuity of the forms of capital consisting in machinery and plant required to assist in forwarding piano production at the different points, by moving on the more or less finished forms of machinery towards the condition of completed machines, so as to satisfy the constant requirements.[1]

[1] It is, of course, not strictly true that the same amount of production always requires the same amount of forms of machinery to assist. New inventions and improvements in the arts constantly vary the number of forms of machinery required to do any given total of work. But, in dealing with the broad general results of demand for commodities, it is necessary to assume a stable condition of the arts, just as we assume a stable condition of demand.

The following illustration may perhaps serve to make the point clear. The long straight line refers to the progress of raw material of pianos towards the complete pianos as a shop good; the short parallel lines refer to the machinery and plant required in the earlier stages of production.

R. M. ——	R. M.^{1} ——	R. M.^{2} ——	GOODS. ——	G.^{1} ——	SHOP GOODS. ——	COM.
Wood, Iron, etc.	Wood, Iron, etc., partly wrought.	Wood, Iron, etc., worked into parts of Pianos.	Pianos.	Pianos in Merchant's hands.	Pianos in Retailer's hands.	Pianos in Consumer's hands.
|	|	|	|			
Machinery.	Machinery.	Machinery.	Machinery.			
|	|	|	|			
Imperfect Machinery.	Imperfect Machinery.	Imperfect Machinery.	Imperfect Machinery.			
|	|	|	|			
More Imperfect Machinery.	More Imperfect Machinery.	More Imperfect Machinery.	More Imperfect Machinery.			
|	|	|	|			
R. M. of Machinery.	R. M. of Machinery.	R. M. of Machinery.	R. M. of Machinery.			

It will be evident from the previous argument that my demand for a piano to pass from the last stage in production, viz., shop goods into commodity, sets in operation a force which acts not only at every point, along the direct line from R. M. to Com., but at every point in each of the perpendicular lines, impelling the raw material of machinery to advance one step towards finished machinery. It is needless to remark that the effect of my exercise of demand on the perpendicular lines is extremely slight as compared with the effect on the straight line of production, inasmuch as the wear and tear of machinery in assisting to produce one piano would be extremely small, but, for all that, the effort should not be overlooked. The regular demand for pianos keeps in continuous existence an equal number of forms of piano material at various stages, and an equal number of forms of plant and machinery. We have taken here the instance of the piano trade, but what holds there holds of trade in general. If we neglect the specific piano element in the above illustration, and read it to indicate the whole mechanism of commerce which is concerned in promoting the production of utilities and conveniences, we shall see that demand for commodities gives continuity and employment to the whole machine.

Thus we see that not only does the exercise of demand for commodities fail to diminish the real capital stationed at the various stages in production, but that it keeps in continuous existence the same quantity of capital in the various shapes necessary.

Each individual form of capital perishes, but only on condition that the spirit which has animated it pass into another form, which performs a service like unto the former one. This continuity of capital is analogous to the continuity of a community ; each individual dies in his turn, but the community is the same; each individual continually grows older, but the average age of the individual in the community remains the same, and there are always the same proportion of individuals at any given age. Or the individual forms of capital may be likened to drops of water in a river ; each in turn passes down the course and is lost in the ocean, but the river never grows less, its continuity is never lost.

Thus far the argument has brought us to two important conclusions. First, that in a condition of steady consumption the continuous existence of capital, and of the same number of forms of capital, is maintained by a force which owes its impetus to a constant demand for commodities. Second, that the profits which form the money incomes of all capitalists concerned in production, the wages of all the labourers concerned, and the rent of all the natural agents required, are, in a regular condition of commerce, paid out of the prices paid by consumers, that is, out of retail prices.

Before we pass from investigating the results of a normal rate of demand for commodities to an examination of the effects of a growing rate of demand, it will be well to draw attention to one or two conclusions which may be regarded as corollaries of the argument above.

(A.) It has been often asserted that labourers are maintained out of capital; that they eat, drink, and wear capital, replacing its value by productive labour.

Since the definition of capital here accepted excludes all commodities, it will be obvious that the food, clothing, &c., enjoyed by labourers is no part of the capital of the community.

But since it still appears to be held by some economists that an individual capitalist owns a 'sustentation fund,' which to all intents consists of food, clothing, shelter, and that he provides labourers with these desirable things while they are labouring, it may be well to state distinctly the facts. Labourers do not receive wages until they have embodied the value of their wages in new products. But if the capitalist obtains a new value of £. 1 before he parts with £. 1 in the form of wages, it is evident that the £. 1 paid to his labourer is no part of the capitalist's capital. At the beginning of the week, if the capitalist possessed this sovereign, it will rightly have been regarded as a portion of his capital. But his capital, so far as it was embodied in the sovereign, has now moved out of that embodiment into something wholly or partly produced by his labourer. Thus, if a capitalist possesses £. 100, and buys labour, at the end of the week he possesses the value produced by the labour; his capital is now embodied in this newly produced value, and no part of his capital is paid to the labourers when he pays them the £. 100. The labourers have produced £. 100 value, and receive £. 100 in exchange; the capitalist still retains his £. 100 capital, though in an altered shape.

If there is in no case an advance of wages on the part of the capitalist, and if the act of paying wages is an act of exchange by which the capitalist becomes possessed of certain value created by the labourer, for which he pays an agreed price (wages), whence comes the notion of a sustentation fund? The answer would appear to be this: a capitalist, to conduct his business successfully, must have his capital stored in different shapes. Part of it is in the shape of machinery and other plant, part of it in the shape of raw material, and raw material in each and every stage in which it is his business to deal with it. Now, when he starts in business, he will purchase his machinery and plant and his raw material; but, as he does not yet possess raw material in every stage up to goods, his capital is not complete. To supply himself with these further forms of capital, he has to purchase labour to advance raw material till he possesses it in every stage. For some weeks, therefore, he must have a fund of money out of which he can continuously purchase the labour necessary to advance his raw material to the various stages necessary to make his capital complete. These labourers at first sight appear to be subsisted out of a sustentation fund possessed by the capitalist, and this idea has been seized on by some economists and elaborated into a sort of incipient wages-fund theory; it is, however, evident that this is wholly unjustifiable. The capitalist possesses certain capital, money (or we may say certain capital, food, and necessaries of labourers), and this form, or these forms, of capital he wishes to exchange for forms suitable to the conduct of his business; he, therefore, agrees to exchange them with labourers for the labour requisite to convert his raw material into a line of raw material in every stage of production up to the goods he sells. So soon as his capital is complete his weekly sales of goods provide him with the money requisite to pay his labourers' weekly wages, his rent, and his own profit. All, therefore, that the capitalist possesses is the capital requisite to carry on his business; no funds of any sort are set apart as a sustentation fund.

But it will, perhaps, be objected that there is an element of risk in all production; the result may turn out to have no market value, or the forms in which the labour is stored may be accidentally destroyed; these risks, it will, perhaps, be said, are undertaken by the capitalist, and involve the necessity of his possessing a sustentation fund, out of which his labourers' wages may at such periods be paid. But on examination this contention is seen to be equally baseless with that already examined. The capitalist in each of these cases has purchased from the labourers a certain total of labour, and pays in money for this labour. If the capitalist has directed the labourers to embody their labour in useless forms, or if, though embodied in useful forms, he does not guard against their accidental destruction, he has in either case lost a portion of his capital. The capital has not been given to, and consumed by, the labourers, but the particular forms in which it exists have, in the first case, no market value, and in the other have been destroyed. The labourers sold a certain specific total of labour for a certain specific price, and the purchase and payment is exactly equivalent to the purchase and payment for the use of land or capital. Though individuals may, and frequently do, lose 'money' by hiring a farm, no one suggests that a landowner is subsisted out of a sustentation fund, and because individuals may similarly lose money by hiring labourers, it is equally absurd to suggest that this proves them to be subsisted out of a sustentation fund.

But it will, perhaps, be suggested that, as sales of goods are more or less irregular, the capitalist must possess a sustentation fund, out of which to pay his labourers' wages at any period when the sale of his goods temporarily ceases. Though the arguments we have used really answer this objection, it is as well to glance briefly at it. What has really happened in this case is, that the capitalist has put part of his capital into temporarily useless forms. To conduct his business he must, therefore, be provided with certain additional capital. Thus, if we assume he requires £.20,000 of forms of capital to conduct his business, but, owing to lack of foresight, occasionally gets £.5,000 into temporarily useless forms, then he must have £.25,000 forms of capital in all. Did he possess perfect foresight he would never purchase any labour other than that requisite to enable him to just finish the production of the articles he sells at the exact moment when they are sold, and in this case he would only require £.20,000 of forms of capital. Owing to the fact that capitalists possess varying degrees of foresight, the quantity of capital required by them for the due conduct of any business varies; but this does not afford any grounds for resuscitating any part of the wages fund doctrine under a new name, but merely shows that more capital is actually requisite than would be the case if capitalists were endowed with perfect foresight.

The fact of certain additional capital being requisite may, perhaps, suggest that this capital is of the nature of a 'risk fund,' but, if so, the 'risk fund' is not paid away to the labourers as wages. The capitalist still possesses his risk fund intact; true, he has directed his labourers to embody it in a temporarily useless form, but none the less it is as wholly and absolutely his as before the purchase of the labour. This being the case it is obvious that no fraction of this 'risk fund' has been paid away to the labourers.

We may conclude, therefore, that labourers are paid out of the value they assist in producing. Their wages are their share of this value, and their wages are no more advanced from any special fund than the landlord's rent or the capitalist's profit.[1] It is, of course, evident that 'sustentation fund' may be defined so as to cover the whole fund which is divisible as income among the members of the community. If so defined, we have no objection to it; it is only when used to differentiate the source of labourers' incomes from the source of the incomes of other members of the community, and to embody part or all of the wages fund doctrine, that it is necessary to object to it.

(B.) Capital is not consumed in the wear and tear of machinery, but constantly passes out of disused or worn-out forms into new forms.

Karl Marx has argued that machinery is worked up into the products it helps to produce, and is thus consumed in the commodities. He wishes to maintain the claim of living present labour to be the sole productive agent; hence he maintains that the only service done by machinery consists in the value it

[1] For the similar conclusion of Marx, see his "Capital," Part VII. Ch. XXIII.

adds to raw materials by being worked up in conjunction with it to form commodities. Thus the reward paid to a machinery owner ought not to exceed the total cost of production of the machine.

In reply to this we may briefly urge :—

1. That it is not literally true that the material of the machine passes into the commodity.
2. That if the statement is to be understood metaphorically, it is equally true of the labourer. He is used up to make commodities, and the sum of wages received during his life should, in accordance with Marx's argument, not exceed his cost of production. This last element in a slave community would be easily ascertained.
3. It has been shown that the real capital, either from the point of view of the community or of the individual capitalist, is not for one moment diminished by the constant process of wear and tear. His capital is not worked up into anything, but remains intact and embodied in the same number of various forms all the time.

While the community is unable to consume its capital, to consume its fields, railways, factories, steam-engines, shops, and iron foundries, to eat its growing corn, or wear its unspun cotton and unwoven wool, the individual suffers from no such disability. He can convert his fields or houses, his ironworks or growing crops, into champagne and truffles with the utmost facility. To explain the apparent paradox, that any individual can accomplish what the aggregate of all individuals cannot accomplish, it is only necessary to consider what the aggregate consumable income of the community actually is. This consumable income is the annual output of 'subsistence, conveniences, and amusements;' this is the sum total of what the community actually receives in exchange for its various efforts and labours. The individual's income is the particular share of this total to which such individual is, under the present social arrangements, entitled. Thus, the aggregate of all individuals' incomes exactly equals the community's income. Now, since the community, as a whole, can never consume more 'subsistence, conveniences, and amusements' than it has actually produced, it is obvious that the community[1] can never live beyond its income. If, therefore, any given individual wishes to live beyond his income, he can only do so provided that some other individual or individuals will consent to consume as much less of their income or incomes as he wishes to consume more, and will hand over to him this excess in exchange for the machinery or raw material which he possesses. Thus the extravagant individual consumes his neighbours' incomes, whilst these thrifty neighbours become possessed of the capital which he previously owned. Therefore, although it is usual to speak of an individual as consuming or living upon his capital, it is evident that this is, so far as the community is concerned, not accurate. No capital is destroyed; all that happens is that certain capital which previously belonged to A. has been transferred to B., and certain income

[1] It may here be well to remind the reader again that community means the whole industrial public. A nation, as an individual, may live beyond its income for a time.

accumulated by B. as savings has been transferred to A. and consumed by him.

Having thus seen that in no case can the community's capital be demanded and consumed, we have next to ascertain what is meant by the common term 'demand for capital.' When A. offers at the end of the year to repay to B. £.105 for every £.100 B. now lends A., he is said to demand capital. It is, however, obvious that this term is incorrectly applied. A. does not obtain any part of B.'s capital; all that he gets is the use of £.100 of it for one year. Similarly, A. does not give B. £.105; for of this sum £.100 is, and always has been, B.'s; all he gives B. is £.5. What really has happened is, therefore, that A. obtains the use of B.'s £.100 for one year, and pays for this use £.5. Now this £.5 is called interest; interest, therefore, is payment for the use of money.

Similarly, when A. hires a cotton factory from B., and agrees not merely to maintain it in good repair, to replace all worn-out machinery by new, &c., but, in addition, to give B. £.500 a-year, this £.500 is paid for the use of B.'s capital. B. never parts with the ownership of any part or fraction of his factory; all that A. gets is the use of it, and for this use he pays B. £.500. If, in addition, A. borrows the raw material and other funds requisite to enable him to work the factory, and promises to return all those funds to B. at the end of the year, together with a sum of £.500, then it is obvious that this £.500 is paid to B. as the price of the use of B.'s capital. These prices are demand for the use of capital, and in commercial language are known as interest, profit, or rent; the first of these terms being applied to the demand for the use of money, the second to the demand for the use of raw material, goods, &c., and the third to the demand for the use of factories, warehouses, stores, houses, &c.; in fact, to all forms of capital with which any portion of natural agents are inseparably connected. We need not, however, trouble ourselves with any elaborate discussion of the propriety of these terms. All we have to insist on is the central fact, that each and all of these funds are paid for the use either of capital or of natural agents; that they are the demand for the use of capital or natural agents.

Returning now to the main purport of our argument, we have next to examine the effect of an increasing demand for commodities in its relation to a fixed supply. The generally accepted economic law of market price is this: 'That when the demand for an article tends to exceed the supply, the price rises; when the supply tends to exceed the demand, the price falls.' To this statement of the law there are two objections. First, a tendency towards such excess could have no result; no producer will put up his price until he actually has, or believes that he will shortly have, more bids at current prices than he can supply. Secondly, the use of the word 'demand' here is particularly ambiguous, as it seems to denote either the amount of desire to possess on the part of consumers, or the quantity of money which they would pay at present prices to satisfy this desire.

Now, there is no common measure by which desire may be related to the quantity of supply, so that the first meaning of 'demand' will not be of any service.

On the other hand, to say that price varies as the quantity of money offered varies in relation to a fixed supply, is no law of price, but merely an expansion of the statement that 'price varies.' The true relation involved in the law of price is between quantity demanded and quantity offered, *i.e.*, supply, and the exact statement of the law is as follows: 'When the quantity demanded in the present exceeds the quantity demanded in the past, in relation to a fixed supply, prices rise; when the quantity demanded in the present falls below that demanded in the past, prices fall.' This is the simplest statement of the mode of price change. Whatever economic causes, such as increase or decrease in cost of production, affect prices, will be found to operate through the medium of changes in the relation of quantity demanded and supply.

It is indeed obvious that so long as sellers can sell everything they wish to sell at the current price, they will resolutely refuse to take less than this price; so long, therefore, as the quantity demanded does not decrease relatively to supply, the price cannot fall. It is equally obvious that if sellers cannot clear everything they wish to sell at the current price, they will sooner or later consent to accept less than this price rather than continue to accumulate an unsold surplus; so soon, therefore, as the quantity demanded decreases relatively to supply, prices will fall.

Similarly, if sellers find that they could sell more than they have to offer at the current price, they will raise their prices. The seller wishes to get the highest price possible consistent with selling all the goods he has to offer, and he will only cease raising his prices when he finds he can only just effect this object. So soon, therefore, as the quantity demanded increases relatively to supply, the price must rise.

It will doubtless be urged that we are here taking merely a superficial and altogether too simple a view of price. Instead of asking the immediate cause of a rise or fall, we should seek its ultimate cause, and wander back into the mazes and mysteries of normal price, cost of production, and the various other abstractions which have proved a veritable Serbonian bog to adventurous economists. But our particular object in reaching a law of price does not require an exploration of these remote and doubtful regions; it is sufficient for us to know that if the price of any article falls, this fall demonstrates that the quantity of such articles demanded has decreased relatively to the quantity offered for sale. If it be admitted that any producer who can sell all he has to offer at the current price, will absolutely refuse to take less than this price, it must also be admitted that if the price falls it demonstrates that producers offer more such articles for sale than purchasers will buy at the old price. Were it not so, why should producers take less? But if it be so then a fall in price shows that supply has increased relatively to quantity demanded.[1]

We have next to consider what takes place when any community increases its rate of consumption, as, for instance, the United States is now doing. Does this constantly increasing consumption empty the shops and warehouses, deplete the stocks in hands of manufacturers, and sweep the flocks and herds from the broad plains of the far West? The answer is

[1] The arguments of the currency school of Economists are dealt with in Ch. VII.

known to the world, it does none of these things; the growth in consumption is accompanied by a corresponding growth in retail and wholesale stocks, in raw material undergoing the processes of manufacture, and by an equal or more than equal increase in the flocks and herds, in the land under cultivation, and in all the plant and machinery of manufacture, of transport, of storage and retailing. Whilst, however, these broad facts are matters of general knowledge, and have been quantitatively related to each other in Chapter II., it is desirable to ascertain the link which in actual commerce connects these two phenomena (increasing consumption and increasing capital). This link is to be found in price.

Before a consumer can consume any article he must buy it, and the price which he pays must always on the average suffice—

a. To enable the retailer to purchase a new and in all respects equivalent article from the manufacturer.

b. To pay all the expenses incidental to the storage and sale, and, in addition, to yield him such a profit as will induce him to keep a sufficient stock of such articles to enable consumers to effect their purchases.

It is evident that no retailer would sell an article in current demand unless the price he receives will enable him to buy a new and equivalent article from the makers. For instance, a hatter would not sell a hat for ten shillings if he had at once to pay eleven shillings to the maker for a new hat to replace the one sold. In addition to this, it is evident that the price he receives must repay his outlay on rent and wages, and must also yield him a sufficient profit to induce him to apply his capital and energies to the trade. Did it not suffice for these purposes, the retailers would not keep a stock, and if they did not keep a stock consumers could not buy and consume. But if each purchase must always provide the retailer with sufficient funds to replace the article sold, and, in addition, repay all his expenses and leave him a profit sufficient to induce him to keep the requisite stock of such articles, no matter how vigorously consumers may press their demands, they will never deplete his stock. This stock is, we can see, protected by the price he charges, and this price is an effective guarantee that no undue consumption should ever take place. This is no mere theoretical conclusion; it is a truism of commerce. The more any retailer's trade increases, the larger will be the stock he keeps. Instances are within everyone's experience. The trade of a particular shop or locality increases, and with every such increase comes an enlargement of premises and an increase in the quantity of stock offered for sale.

The argument which applies to retailers applies equally to manufacturers; taking the price received by the manufacturer, that is to say, portion *a* of the retail price, we find that this price is likewise divisible into two parts, it must suffice—

c. To enable the manufacturer to replace the raw material of his trade;

d. To pay all the expenses of manufacture (wages and rent), and, in addition, yield the manufacturer such a profit as will induce him to apply his capital and energies to the trade.

It is evident that no manufacturer will usually and habitually sell an article in current demand for less than it costs to produce. If at the present price of cotton yarns, the present rates of wages and rent, &c., it costs him one shilling to make a yard of calico, he will not sell a yard of calico for ten pence. But even if he could get one shilling a yard, he would not consent to trade on these terms; in addition to this one shilling he must receive a profit that will induce him to apply his capital and energies to the trade. Now, so soon as he finds that he could obtain this profit on a larger output of goods, he will seek to borrow or otherwise obtain the use of the funds requisite to enable him to enlarge his manufactory and to increase the quantities of raw material undergoing manufacture. This increase in his manufacturing operations involves the purchase of new machinery, &c., the erection of new buildings, &c., and not impossibly the construction of new means of communication (railways, ships, and the like). Whilst the replacement of worn-out machinery is a comparatively trifling matter, the creation of new plant to supply an increase in consumption requires no small proportion of the productive energies of a community. The plant required to produce any individual commodity by modern methods vastly exceeds in value the individual commodity itself, and we certainly do not over-estimate this difference if we assume that an increase of ten per cent. in the annual consumption of any community would require an increase of fifty per cent. in the production of that community during the year of increase.

If, for instance, the increase in consumption takes the form of bread or meat, it will be necessary to bring fresh land into cultivation, to fence and drain it, make roads and bridges, build barns, stables, and farmhouses, and to provide the means of transport, &c., &c. It will further be necessary to build mills for grinding the larger total of wheat, to construct new bakehouses and additional shops for its baking and distribution, and similarly with meat. The value embodied in all these various classes of plant will vastly exceed the value of a week's or even of a year's output of the bread and meat they have assisted to produce. So soon, however, as the new forms of capital have been once created, a continuance of the increased consumption would only require the corresponding ten per cent. increase in production. Thus, if a community increases its consumption from 10 x wealth to 11 x wealth a year, production must during the year when this increase takes place exceed consumption by 4 x wealth in order to accumulate the additional forms of capital required; that is to say, production must during this year amount to 15 x wealth. So soon, however, as consumption, having reached 11 x wealth annually, no longer increases, a production of 11 x wealth annually is alone required.[1] We thus see that the quantitative relation between capital and consumption which we showed in Chap. II. must exist, is maintained through the medium of price and profit.

If it be objected that perhaps no capital may be available to increase the powers of production at the various stages, or that production is limited, not by capital, but by the quantity of natural agents or of

[1] Repairs of existing machinery and other forms of plant are paid for out of the prices of the commodities they assist in producing, and must be regarded as part of the production of those commodities.

labour available for use, then we reply, no increase in consumption is possible. Retailers being unable to replace the articles sold will raise their prices until the quantity demanded is brought into proper economic relation with supply. The fact that in such communities as the United States consumption is rapidly increasing simultaneously with an equally rapid increase in its capital, demonstrates that the capital can be accumulated. Our present inquiry is, therefore, limited to ascertaining how the quantitative relation between these two quantities (consumption and capital) is maintained. We do not make the ridiculous assertion that consumption can always increase, but merely that if it increases capital will of necessity simultaneously increase.

The fact that a price is paid guarantees that the consumption of the article purchased shall in no wise deplete capital. It guarantees that in no case shall consumption exceed the total that is economically desirable. When, however, consumption is effected without the payment of a price, as, for instance, by the devastation of war, by the exactions of a conqueror or a tyrant, then these guarantees are lacking, and consumption may and probably will deplete capital.

We might carry on this analysis of trade till we reached the producers of the raw material, and we should then find that the whole of the price received by them was divisible as rent, wages, and profit or interest, but the argument is so simple and obvious that no advantage would be gained by so doing.

Similarly, when we consider a decreasing consumption, it is evident that as the retailers' sales decrease, their profits decrease, and with every such decrease the inducement to keep stock decreases. Thus, when we find a shop or town suffering from a rapid decline of trade, this decline does not cause an accumulation of stock, but, on the contrary, the stock offered for sale decreases more or less in proportion.

The same holds good of the manufacturer. If a manufacturer finds his sales decreasing, he decreases the quantities of raw material under treatment, and does not even maintain the whole of his plant in efficient repair. Every contraction in the quantity demanded, therefore, operating through price and profit, reduces the stock of shop goods and raw material, and causes portions of the existing plant to be no longer maintained. No matter how much capital may be available for use, the inducement to use it depends exclusively on the demand for commodities, and if this demand decreases a force is set in operation which, working through price and profit at each stage in the process of production, decreases the quantity of forms of capital in existence. This decrease is in no wise due to any difficulty in maintaining and keeping these forms in order or in replacing them by new ones, but is due exclusively to the fact that no one has any inducement to maintain them or to replace them by new ones.

Although it has been shown in the preceding argument that the money income of the community, being composed of the margins of gain at different points in the productive process, varies with consumption, it is important to identify the actual money paid by consumers for commodities as the ultimate source of all incomes. If we consider the individual in a community, it is evident that his income is received by him as payment for the use of that requisite of production which he owns. If he be a labourer, he receives his income (wages) as a demand for the use of his labour; if he owns land, mines, &c., he receives his income (rent) as payment for the use of the same; if he owns capital, he receives his income (profit) as payment for the use of his capital.

Directly or indirectly every individual's income is derived from one or other of these funds; whether he be mortgagee or annuitant, shareholder or what not, his income can invariably be referred back, either to the rent of a natural agent, to the profit on capital, or to the wages of labour.[1]

The individual sells a given total of the use of a requisite of production owned by him, and the price he receives for this use is his income. Thus the land-owner sells the use of his land for a year, and the price he receives for this use is his income (rent). The labourer sells the use of his mental and bodily abilities for a day, a week, or a year, and the price he receives for this use is his income (wages). The capitalist sells the use of his capital, and the price he receives for this use is his income (profit or interest). Since, however, every individual's income may be referred back to one or other of these funds,[2] it follows that the sum of these prices is the aggregate money income of the community. That is to say the aggregate demand, or prices paid, for the use of the requisites of production is the aggregate money income of all the individuals composing the community.

[1] We include under the head of wages all payments made for services, those of the highly-trained professional man equally with those of the mechanic.

[2] We are here again following Prof. Cairnes, who shows that all incomes are necessarily derived from production. (See 'Some Leading Prin. Pol. Ec.,' Chap. II.)

It has already been seen that consumption of commodities is the ultimate cause which determines the extent of the use of these requisites of production. It remains, therefore, only to illustrate more precisely in what way the payment for these uses of requisites of production is derived from the payment for commodities by consumers. So far as the actual money received as income by the owners of requisites of production is concerned, there is little difficulty. This money received as income is continually applied to purchase shop-goods, and is paid into the till of retail traders; these traders pay in their cash to the banks, daily or weekly, and this cash is again withdrawn by capitalists, and applied by them to pay wages, rent, and profit. To illustrate more clearly the actual series of payments that take place, we will assume that a certain town spends £.30,000 a-week in bread; the £.30,000, we may assume, will be distributed as follows :—

	£.		£.
Bakers receive weekly for bread - and pay weekly to millers for flour, £. 20,000.	30,000	All concerned in the baking and retailing of bread receive weekly as income - - -	10,000
Millers receive weekly for flour from bakers - - - - and pay weekly to merchants for corn, £. 18,000.	20,000	All concerned in the milling of the wheat - - - -	2,000
Merchants receive weekly for corn from millers - - - and pay weekly to farmers for corn, £. 17,000.	18,000	All concerned in the transport and warehousing of the corn -	1,000
Farmers receive weekly for corn, £. 17,000 from merchants -	17,000	All concerned in the growing, threshing, &c., of the wheat -	17,000
			30,000

We thus see that the whole £.30,000 is distributed as rent, wages, and profit amongst all concerned in the production of the commodity bread. The baker pays the miller, and the miller the merchant, and the merchant the farmer simultaneously. The baker draws a cheque for £. 20,000, which he gives to the miller; the miller draws a cheque for £. 18,000, which he gives to the merchant; and the merchant a cheque for £. 17,000, which he gives to the farmer. But it may be asked, How can all these cheques be met? There are only 30,000 sovereigns, and cheques are drawn for £. 55,000. The answer is clear. The baker, having drawn a cheque for £. 20,000, must pay in to his banker £. 20,000 out of his £. 30,000, retaining merely £. 10,000 with which to pay the rent of his bakehouse, shop, &c., the wages of his men, and his own profits and wages. The miller, who receives £. 20,000, having to meet his cheque of £. 18,000 paid to the merchant, cannot draw in cash more than £. 2,000; with this £. 2,000 he must pay his rent, men's wages, and his own income. The merchant, having to meet the cheque for £. 17,000 he has given the farmer, can only draw £. 1,000, and out of this sum he must pay for the transport of the wheat, rent of his stores, &c., and his own income. The farmer, however, has no cheque to meet, so he can devote his whole £. 17,000 to the payment of rent, labourers' wages, and his own income.

The only sums in money withdrawn from the bank are, therefore, the miller's £. 2,000, the merchant's £. 1,000, and the farmer's £. 17,000; that is to say, that exact £. 20,000 paid in by the baker to meet his cheque for that sum. These sums are evidently the demand or purchasing power exerted for the use of the various requisites of production concerned in the production of bread. If we assume the demand for bread suddenly increased by one-half, it is clear that each of these totals would be increased simultaneously; the baker would have to buy more flour, the miller more wheat, the merchant more wheat, and the farmer would find himself provided with the funds requisite to hire more land and labour. It may, perhaps, be urged that the farmer cannot supply more wheat than formerly. In that case the merchant, the miller, and the baker will each and all be limited to the sale of the old amount of wheat, flour, and bread; the increased demand will expend itself in raising the price, and though the farmer sells no more wheat than before, he will receive the additional funds requisite to enable him to increase his purchases of the use of land and labour.

Mill rightly contended that the demand for shop goods was not the demand for the labour which had previously produced them, because the money I pay to-day cannot have provided the wages which were paid last year to the man who sowed the particular grains of wheat from which my loaf has sprung. But while it is true that the present demand for shop goods is not the source from which past demand for labour proceeded, it by no means follows that present demand for shop goods is not the source of present demand for labour. Take the case of a tanner, who is also a shoe manufacturer and a retailer. The only money he can receive is from the custom of his retail shop, *i.e.*, is the demand for boots. With this money he pays the weekly wages of his 'shoe hands,' his 'leather finishers and dressers,' his 'yard-hands,' and all concerned in the preparation of the leather and its manufacture into boots. Part of the money he receives daily as demand for boots he distributes daily as demand for the use of labour. If the demand for boots decreased, his demand for the use of labour must necessarily decrease. If, on the other hand, it increased, he would want more boots got ready, more leather dressed, and more hides tanned, and he would be provided with the funds requisite to hire the additional labour required. The money which his workmen receive as wages is part of the money which his customers pay for boots. The demand for boots is the source from which his labourers' wages, his landlord's rent, and his own income are drawn.

It is clear in the above case that rent, profits, and wages are not paid by the tanner out of any fund either of money or other property he has previously become possessed of, but out of the proceeds of each week's production. That is to say, the value put into raw material is divided up when each piece of raw material reaches the stage of commodity, and the proceeds of the division are paid as rent, profit, wages. The fact that rent, profit, wages are not paid in boots but in general purchasing power does not impair the value of this statement, for general purchasing power is only effective on the supposition that a steady work of production has been carried on in other branches of industry similar in character to the work of the tanning trade.

Or, again, to illustrate the same point, let us take the whole work of a community conducted according to an ideally uniform pattern. Let us assume that every commodity has passed through ten processes, occupying each a day, before it is finished, and that the demand for each kind of commodity does not vary from day to day, so that at the end of each day's labour there are just so many loaves (or potential loaves) in each of the ten stages which must be passed to make a finished loaf, so many coats (or potential coats) in each of the ten stages which must be passed to make a finished coat, and so with every other kind of commodity. Let us further assume that each labourer assists in advancing one piece of wealth each day a single step towards becoming a commodity. Lastly, suppose labour and capital contribute equally towards the daily advance. Then each body of ten labourers, working in conjunction with capital, will bring one piece of wealth each day into a state of commodity, and will (or should) receive one-half at the end of the day in wages. Each man will thus get one-twentieth of a commodity as his day's wage, the capitalist also receiving one-twentieth for each labourer employed. If we now suppose that each commodity is handed over to consumers as soon as produced, there will be at the beginning of each day no finished products in the hands of the capitalist. The latter will simply have his plant and raw material in all stages short of commodity. In such a community it would be obvious that the commodities paid as profit and wages were paid out of the results of the production of each day. It is true that nine-tenths of the value of the actual commodities handed over in profit and wages at the end of the day was created in the nine previous days, but it is only handed over on condition of having been replaced by an equivalent value stored in other forms of wealth on their way to become commodities. Here the whole of the commodities given as profit and wages are in effect the creation of the one day's work.

The demand for labour and use of capital is here obviously constituted by the commodities daily produced. The requisites of production owned by the labourers and capitalist daily produce a certain total of value, and this total of value is daily distributed to all concerned as payment for the use of these requisites. The labourers and capitalist daily demand 'one piece of wealth,' and this 'one piece of wealth' daily demands the use of the requisites of production owned by them. That is to say, the demand for commodities, and the demand for use of requisites of production is the same phenomenon regarded from different points of view.

In short, the use of natural agents, capital and labour produces commodities, and demand for these commodities is demand for the use of the requisites of production.

In all periods, therefore, when the rate of consumption does not vary, as assumed in our illustration above, the quantity of commodities demanded is the quantity of the use of the requisites of production demanded, or in other words consumption equals production. Variations in the rate of consumption, however, complicate the problem somewhat. We saw, (p. 85), that when consumption increases, this increase can only take place concurrently with a proportionate increase in capital, an increase which is brought about through the medium of price and profit, and which at any given period is quantitatively related to the increase in consumption.

The quantity of the use of the requisites of

production demanded will during such periods consist —

a. Of the quantity required to produce the commodities demanded.

b. Of the quantity required to produce the additional capital rendered necessary by the increase in *a*.

Though in this case the quantity of commodities demanded is not identical with the quantity of the use of the requisites of production demanded, it nevertheless determines the more or less of this latter quantity. Every increase in *a* involving more than an equivalent increase, and every decrease in *a* involving more than an equivalent decrease in the quantity of the use of the requisites of production demanded.

We saw (p. 88), that every individual receives his income as demand for the use of a requisite of production owned by him, and that the aggregate demand for the use of the requisites of production is the aggregate money income of the community. Each individual's income being the price paid for a given total of the use of a requisite of production owned by him, it follows from the law of price deduced on page 81 that any fall in this price shows that the quantity of such use demanded has decreased relatively to the quantity offered.

We now propose to show that such a fall has taken place. To effect this purpose it is necessary to analyse the phenomenon known as depression in trade.

This depression may be defined as a general reduction in the rate of incomes. Whatever form the particular complaint may take, a little analysis will always reduce it to this. When workmen complain that they cannot get work, it does not mean that they feel an insatiable desire for prolonged hours of toil, but that they want wages and cannot get them. They would even prefer wages without work, if it were possible. Similarly, when the trader complains that 'there is nothing doing,' it does not mean that he derives happiness from the constant and rapid manipulation of his capital, but merely that he wishes for the profit which that proceeding would presumably afford him. And the landowner, likewise, when he asserts that 'the country is going to the dogs,' and that foreign wheat is responsible for this, does not really hate foreign wheat, but only objects to the reduction in rent which such wheat causes. Thus, in each case it is a reduction of income that causes individuals to inveigh against the evil times that have befallen them.

Now, the individual's income, we have seen, is the price paid for a given total of the use of a requisite of production owned by him. This price, we have seen, can only fall if the quantity of such uses demanded has decreased relatively to the supply of such uses offered. Depression in trade is, therefore, a decrease in the quantity of the uses of the requisites of production demanded relatively to the supply available, and is resolvable into an insufficiency in the quantity of the use of the requisites of production demanded. But the quantity of commodities demanded determines the quantity of the uses of the requisites of production demanded; if, therefore, this latter quantity is insufficient, this insufficiency is due exclusively to an insufficiency in the former; that is to say, in consumption. The only cause, however, which can lead to an insufficiency in consumption is the undue exercise of the habit of thrift or saving, and this habit, therefore, and depression in trade are merely different phases of one phenomenon.

Or our argument may be stated in inverse order in the following propositions :—

1. Depression in trade is a general fall in the rate of incomes (*i.e.*, a given total of a requisite of production yields its owner a less income).
2. A general fall in the rate of incomes proves that the quantity of the use of the requisites of production demanded has decreased relatively to the supply.
3. The quantity of the use of the requisites of production demanded is determined by the quantity of commodities demanded (consumption).
4. Consumption would always equal the maximum possible, were it not for the habit of saving or thrift.

Whence we conclude depression in trade and excessive thrift are terms describing different phases of the same phenomenon.

Excluding from consideration the complexities introduced by an increase in the rate of consumption, and consequently in the quantity of capital required, we may summarise our theory thus : the community considered as the recipient of money incomes produces consumable articles ; the community considered as the spender of money incomes buys and consumes these articles. If, owing to its desire to save, it refrains from spending the whole of its money income, the whole of the consumable articles produced cannot be sold. Over-supply is, in consequence, caused, and prices and incomes continually fall until the production of consumable articles is reduced to the total actually consumed.

It is important to note that this conclusion does not rest on abstract theory, but is founded on the admitted commercial fact of depression in trade. The identification of depression in trade with insufficient consumption or excessive thrift is, we venture to assert, unassailable. In Chapter II. we showed that the habit of saving might lead to an insufficiency in the rate of consumption, or, as economists prefer to call it, to over-supply ; in this chapter we have shown that it actually has done so.

This conclusion is of critical importance to the community; it means neither more nor less than that the community could at once and permanently enjoy a larger income. It means that the East-end problem, with its concomitants of vice and misery, is traced to its economic cause, and that this economic cause is the most respectable and highly extolled virtue of thrift.

CHAPTER IV.

OVER-PRODUCTION AND ECONOMIC CHECKS.

MOST modern economists deny that consumption could by any possibility be insufficient. To suggest that there may be an excess of forms of capital, over-production of goods, general fall of prices, reduction of incomes, and all the evils on which we have dwelt, is regarded as an absurdity too obvious to need refutation. Is it reasonable to assume that any community will be so foolish as to attempt to save too much? Can we find any economic force at work which might incite a community to this excess, and if there be any such forces are there not efficient checks provided by the mechanism of commerce? These are the questions asked by economists, and to which the present chapter provides an answer.

It will be shown, firstly, that in every highly organised industrial society there is constantly at work a force which naturally operates to induce excess of thrift; secondly, that the checks alleged to be provided by the mechanism of commerce are either wholly inoperative or are inadequate to prevent grave commercial evil. But before setting closely to this task, it is necessary to draw attention to the extreme negligence and indifference with which most modern writers have treated the theory of General Over-production. So firm is their confidence in the value of the automatic machinery of commerce that they are unable to listen with patience to any criticism of the construction of that machinery. If anything goes wrong with the working, there is a system of checks and balances which will be sure to set it right again, or, at any rate, prevent the evil from becoming serious. Hence they have deemed it necessary to do little more than assign a casual recognition to what they call the exploded doctrine of Over-production.

It appears to them a mere absurdity to suppose that in a community where the only possible motive to produce is the desire to consume, an increase in production will not at once be followed by a corresponding increase in consumption. The wants of mankind are infinite; if you increase the amount that can be produced, you increase, *ipso facto*, the amount that will be consumed. The brief answer which Ricardo gave to the contentions of Malthus and Chalmers seems to have been accepted as sufficient by most later economists. "Productions are always bought by productions or by services; money is only the medium by which the exchange is effected. Hence the increased production being always accompanied by a correspondingly increased ability to get and consume, there is no possibility of Over-production."[1] That

[1] Ricardo, 'Prin. of Pol. Econ.,' p. 362.

Commodities are purchased by Commodities, and that along with everything that is produced the power to purchase and consume it is produced have become mere commonplaces of economics.[1] But it must be observed that a further assumption underlies Ricardo's argument, viz., that the power to purchase which is produced must always be exercised. The old notion that it was possible for goods to remain unpurchased and unconsumed because there was no money to buy them, has disappeared before a clearer understanding of the function of money. But though this power to purchase and consume whatever is produced always exists, is it equally certain that this power must always be exerted? To the question put in this form it will be readily replied that a certain portion of the Power to Purchase commodities must be withheld in order that sufficient saving may occur to provide any new capital which may be required to meet any

[1] This argument is specifically adopted by Mill, who says: 'What constitutes the means of payment for commodities is simply commodities. Each person's means of paying for the productions of other people consists of those which he himself possesses. All sellers are inevitably, and by the meaning of the word, buyers. Could we suddenly double the productive powers of the country, we should double the supply of commodities in every market; but we should, by the same stroke, double the purchasing power. Everybody would bring a double demand as well as supply; everybody would be able to buy twice as much, because everyone would have twice as much to offer in exchange.' (Mill, 'Prin. Pol. Ec.,' Book III., Chap. XIV., s. 2.) To this Prof. Marshall, alone amongst economists, takes exception, and pertinently remarks: 'But though men have the power to purchase, they may not choose to use it.' ('Economics of Industry,' Book III., Chap. I., s. 4.) But he fails to grasp the critical importance of this fact, and appears to limit its action to periods of 'crisis.'

expected increase in Consumption.[1] But with the exception of this needful provision for future production, the whole of what is produced must always be consumed. If we ask why it must be consumed, we are met once more with the answer that it is absurd to suppose that people will go on producing unless they consume what they produce, when the only end or object of work is the satisfaction of wants. Thus, the very fact that people produce is proof positive that the Power to Purchase and consume what they produce is actually exercised. "The error is in not perceiving that though all who have an equivalent to give *might* be fully provided with every consumable article which they desire, the fact that they go on adding to the production proves that that is not actually the case."[2]

"We said before that whoever brings additional commodities to the market, brings an additional power of purchase; we now see that he brings also an

[1] Economists usually assert that saving is necessary to maintain the fixed capital in repair, and to replace such of it as may from time to time be worn out. This is, however, an incorrect use of the word saving; no saving is effected unless the aggregate of capital is increased. If the community at the end of the year only possesses exactly the same total of capital that it had at the beginning, how can it be said to have saved?

[2] Here, again, Mr. Mill's Wage-fund theory comes in as a '*deus ex machinâ*.' Suppose that certain individuals really have more 'Purchasing Power' than they care, either at once or in the future, to use, all they have to do is to apply it 'productively' (?) by adding it to the Wages-fund; the labourers will then consent to use the Purchasing Power instead of them. What would happen if the labourers were content with their previous necessaries Mill never stops to ask. Suppose that they tried to save this Purchasing Power handed on to them, what would happen? Mill seems to assign to Capitalists a monopoly of the folly of saving without any object to gain.

additional desire to consume, since if he had not that desire he would not have troubled himself to produce."[1] This is a complete expression of the rough-and-ready general opinion which pronounces Over-production impossible. It rests entirely upon the correctness of the assumption that the sole motive to production is the desire of the producer to consume what he has produced or what he can get for it. Now, of course, if it were the case that immediately any commodity was produced the person or persons concerned in the production insisted on immediately consuming it or consuming what they could get in exchange for it, it would be impossible to conceive of such a thing as Over-production. It is clear that Robinson Crusoe alone on his island would never produce anything which he did not desire to consume; he would never be guilty of such a folly as Over-production, for his only motive to produce is the desire to consume. But is this equally true of individuals in a fully organised industrial society? Is the only motive which induces them to work the desire to consume what they produce? No! there is another motive present, the desire to save. This is as real an acting motive as the other. But, it will be urged, the desire to save only means a desire to consume at some future time. We reply, Yes; but to consume what? Not as a rule to consume what is saved, or any existing value, but to consume something which shall in the future be produced by the assistance of that which is saved. In a word, the real, direct, immediate object of such production is the establish-

[1] Mill, 'Prin. Pol. Econ.,' III., Chap. IV., s. 3. For the similar view of Mr. F. A. Walker, see his 'Pol. Ec.,' 3rd ed., p. 318.

ment of that which is produced as a source of future income. In order to achieve this object the producer seeks to add this 'Saving' to the total of existing Capital. It should clearly be recognised that though there may be present in his mind an intention to consume in the future the return which this piece of Capital may bring in, the original motive to production was not the desire to consume what was produced or what he could get in exchange for it. Thus the desire of individuals to consume what they produce, considered by itself, furnishes no limitation to their willingness to produce. The desire to save may lead them to increase their rate of production indefinitely beyond the desire for present or immediately future consumption. Mill, then, has no right to conclude that the very fact of a thing being produced is a proof that the power to consume it will be exercised. The desire to save and store up purchasing power is as genuine a motive to production in the individual as the desire of immediate consumption.[1] 'But how will this lend a possibility to Over-production?' It may be urged, 'You have already shown that it is impossible to effectually save more than suffices to minister to future Consumption, why, then, will a community be so foolish as to try to save more than this?' The answer to these questions discloses the fundamental fallacy which underlies the Economist's view of Saving, the assumption that the interests of the Community must always be identical with the interests of its several members. The statement of Adam Smith,[2]

[1] Mr. Walker quite overlooks this in his account of the motives to produce, see his 'Pol. Econ.,' 3rd ed., pp. 318 to 328.

[2] 'Wealth of Nations,' Bk. IV., Chap. II., s. 1.

"What is prudence in the conduct of a private family can scarce be folly in that of a great nation," has been taken too generally for a gospel truth. This view, that a community means nothing more than the addition of a number of individual units, and that the interests of Society can be obtained by adding together the interests of individual members, has led to as grave errors in Economics as in other branches of Sociology. The confident assumption, that if individuals look carefully after their own private interests, the welfare of the whole community will be incidentally secured, is the true explanation of the indifference with which students of the mechanism of commerce have regarded all such criticism of the construction of that machine as is contained in theories of Over-production. Now, it is important to look closely into this assumption, for it does more than explain why economists have slighted all theories of Over-Supply. The disclosure of the falsehood on which this assumption rests will also disclose the existence and nature of that force which gives to Over-Supply an actual existence in the world of commerce.

If the interests of each individual in a community were always identical with the interest of the community there could be no such thing as over-supply. It is impossible to suppose that a company of men, producing in common for the common good, would at any time produce more than was required for consumption in the present or near future. It is, in fact, the clash of interests between the community as a whole and the individual members in respect to Saving, that is the cause of Over-Supply. In order to understand this diversity of interest, it is necessary clearly to ascertain what the limits of available thrift are, for the individual and for society. First, let us look at the individual in respect to the power of Saving. An able and industrious man may be able by working hard for twenty years to retire from business and live during the rest of his life upon his savings; that is to say, he may during the earlier part of his life anticipate the work he would have otherwise been obliged to spread over his whole life. It matters not for our present consideration whether he has kept his Savings in the form of money stored in a stocking at home, or has invested it so as to gain an income. The effect of his action has been to escape the necessity of future labour by an excess of labour in the past.

Doing more work than was sufficient to satisfy his present wants, he gave that extra work to others, receiving in return certain money tokens. The possession of these tokens, which he has hoarded up at home, or invested abroad, so as to increase their number, will enable him, when he retires from business, to compel other people to give him the products of their past labour, or to do actual work for him without his doing any work in return. His past production has provided him with a lien upon future production. He has to all intents and purposes been enabled to store up past labour for future use. But how has he been enabled to effect this? The actual material forms in which his past labour has been stored have not survived during the interval between the exercise of the labour and the future use of it. The fact that others had an immediate use for the forms of his past labour was what enabled him to succeed in storing up the value of his work and using it in the future. If he had been obliged to store up, not the money tokens he received for the immediate use of his work, but the actual forms in which his work stood until he wished after twenty years to use them, or to exchange them for other 'utilities or conveniences,' he would find himself unable to do so, unless he were engaged in work of exceptional durability (such as diamond cutting), and even then changes in fashion and the introduction of cheaper methods of production would be liable to impair the value of his savings. However, by giving up the produce of his labour to some one who has a present use for it, and receiving money tokens in its place, it is possible to escape the necessity of doing any work in the future by a sufficient amount of productive energy in the past. His past work will enable him to obtain any kind of wealth or service in the future without any present exertion on his part.

This is what an individual can do. Can a Community do the same? There is no limit to efficacious thrift on the part of an individual. Is there any limit to the efficacious thrift of a Community? We saw that an individual might so work in the past as to avoid *all* work in the future. Does this hold of a Community? Obviously not. There are certain forms of work which a Community cannot anticipate, certain forms of productive labour which cannot be stored at all.

a. A large part of the labour of producing perishable goods cannot be anticipated. In so far as the term 'perishable' applies in a greater or less degree to all forms of Commodities, this restriction has a general bearing. With regard to the vast amount of labour engaged in producing articles of Food the limitation is almost absolute. The greater part of the work of producing food cannot be stored by the community. The same rule applies in a less degree to the production of clothing and other more enduring forms of material commodities. Rust and moths, the dangers of destruction by fire or other accident, changes of fashion, &c., cause a total or partial loss of value in the case of all kept commodities. Generally, it may be said that such labour can only be antedated within certain time limits, and even then subject to considerable losses.

This consideration imposes an absolute limit on what may be called 'anticipatory production' in a society organised on commercial principles. No man will spend twenty shillings in producing an article for future consumption, if by retaining the twenty shillings and producing the article at a later period immediately prior to its consumption, a larger price can be obtained. It pays better to retain the money and to produce in the future rather than to produce in the present for future consumption.

β. The greater part of that labour, which consists not in imparting new shape or qualities to material objects, but in moving them to the exact place where they are wanted, cannot be anticipated, but requires to be freshly exercised in accordance with the requirements of each moment and each consumer.

γ. Most of that labour which is used to produce non-material commodities is incapable of being stored, *e.g.*, most intellectual or artistic labour, *e.g.*, of Actors,

Singers, Preachers, &c. Under this head may also come most of the work of Domestic Service.

Some forms of intellectual and artistic labour, it is true, may be more effectually stored than any material objects, and may form *κτήματα ἐς ἄει*, but most of the less exalted forms demand constant renewal.

δ. The work of repairing loss of machinery caused by waste or accident cannot be stored.

ε. The whole labour of supplying new wants cannot be stored.

Thus it appears that a large part of the total of productive labour must be done continuously, and is incapable of being stored. A whole community is thus incapable of doing what we saw an individual can do. A community cannot by working extra hard in the present avoid the necessity of doing any work in the future. Our law of Quantitative Relation asserted a fixed relation between the Amount of Present Production and the Amount of Future Consumption. We now further see that this Productive work of providing for Future Consumption cannot be achieved by a series of bursts of productive activity, followed by periods of idleness, that any tendency to this spasmodic action is attended by a loss in the value of the work. It follows, that the economically efficient mode of Production, from the point of view of a Community, is a continuous even exercise of productive energy directed to the supply of immediately future Consumption, and that any attempt on the part of the community to do work before it is economically required must be paid for by a certain loss in the value of the work.

Thus we see that while there is no limit to the effective thrift of an individual, there is a limit to that of the community. But the thrift of the community is composed of the thrift of individuals. It is clear, then, that if the united thrift of individuals passes the limit imposed by the interests of the community, thrift ceases to be as effectual as before, even from the individual's point of view; that is to say, though any individual may anticipate all future labour, every individual cannot. If every individual were seized with a desire to work harder this year in order to have a complete holiday next year, they could not effect this object, though any one or more might succeed in doing so. But though in reality the number of individuals required to do the amount of saving which is economically useful is limited, this restriction does not act as a deterrent in the case of any individual desirous to save. For whether the amount of thrift at present practised in a community is or is not sufficient, the individual can always save. If it is not sufficient, his savings will have a full economic value with the savings of others; if it is sufficient, he runs a certain risk of finding that his savings are not wanted, but he has always the chance of ousting the savings of another.

The only absolute limit to the amount that an individual could save would be the total Capital which the Community can profitably use. It is abstractedly conceivable that an individual or small group of individuals should by thus possessing themselves of the total capital negative all the value of the thrift of other individuals in the community. There is thus nothing to limit the proportion of the total efficient thrift of a community which may be exercised by any individual. If the Community wishes to increase its Capital, it must consent to increase its Consumption; but the individual need not increase his Consumption in order to increase his Capital; indeed, the simplest and most usual method is to decrease his consumption, and this is the method which philanthropists and economists invariably urge. The limitation of National Thrift assigns no absolute limit to the effectiveness of individual thrift. So much Saving can be done by the community, how much of it shall be done by this individual? It is not to the interests of the community that there should be more Saving done than is just sufficient to furnish the requisite quantum of Capital. In a Communistic Society, where the interests of individuals were identical, it is clear that no more Saving would be attempted than this requisite quantity; but the case is different in an individualistic Society. Each is competing against the other; each is seeking to do himself the largest portion of the useful Saving. An individual can always save.

Now, it is just this spirit of competition among individuals which supplies the force that operates to bring about Over-production. If the full number of material forms of machinery, raw material, and goods requisite to complete the economic Capital of the community is already present, is it not still open to the individual to save and create new forms, and apply them so as to oust the forms of his competitors? A certain amount of machinery may be economically required to supply the number of shoes for the retail market. The full amount of this machinery may be already in existence. But that will not prevent me from applying my Saving to the production of other shoemaking machines if I think that I can produce the more efficient machines, which will render useless some of those existing at present and do the work which they would otherwise have done ; or if, with similar machinery, I can produce more cheaply, by using brown paper in the place of leather, or by beating down the wages of my workpeople, and thus force some of the previously existing machinery to stand idle.

It is true that I may fail in my attempt. I may produce machines inferior to those already in use, or otherwise fail to produce more cheaply. In that case I shall have tried to save, have stored up the material forms of Savings, but have effected no real Saving for myself. But whether I succeed or fail, it is clear that my thrift in no wise affects the total economic thrift of the community, but only determines whether a particular portion of the total thrift shall have been exercised by myself or by somebody else. It is, of course, true that the inducement to individuals to save is by no means always the same.[1]

If a community is provided with the smallest number of forms of Capital requisite to supply future Consumption, each of these forms must be considered to have a full and equal value in the aid it renders production ; all parts of the total capital are put to

[1] In Chapter VI. we shall show how the thrift of one part of the community has power to force another part to live beyond their income. See pages 185 and 186.

a full economic use. Since this Capital is the result of previous thrift of individuals, we may say this, that the thrift of individuals has a full and even economic value, and the reward of that thrift will be full and equal. This is what may be termed the normal healthy condition of commerce, where every piece of Savings applied as Capital has a full use, and returns a full profit to its owner. But as soon as competition among individuals leads to the application of a larger number of forms of Capital than are required, it is clear that the average productive work done by each form of Capital is now smaller than before. Either all the forms of Capital are now less fully used than before, or some of the old forms are displaced by new forms, and are no longer used at all. In either case this creation of excessive number of forms of Capital has lowered the average value of each form.

The operation of this spirit of competition among individuals in an industrial community may be fairly illustrated by the conditions of a competitive examination for a limited number of posts or prizes. A dozen posts are offered for open competition to the most successful among fifty candidates, sixty per cent. of marks being required as a qualification. So far as the examination is concerned, it is only requisite that twelve out of the fifty candidates should do enough work to obtain each sixty per cent. of the marks. All the work done in excess of this by the twelve successful candidates and the whole of the work done by the thirty-eight unsuccessful candidates is entirely void of result so far as the examination is concerned; that is to say, if it had not been done, the result would have been just the same. Now, if these candidates were, before they began to prepare for the examination, to come to a mutual agreement with a view to so arranging matters that they should, as a company, do the least possible work consistent with obtaining the desired result, they would select the twelve among them who were at the present time most advanced in attainments, and who could, therefore, presumably be coached most easily, so as to obtain the requisite minimum of marks; these twelve would do what work was required, the other thirty-eight would do no work.

But what occurs under ordinary conditions of competition is this. The consideration of the number of vacant posts and of the minimum of marks required have no limiting effect on the amount of work the candidates do. Each candidate has, or thinks he has, a chance of success, and this chance stimulates him to work. Thus the total of work done is far in excess of that which the conditions of the examination required. It is further to be observed that in proportion as the chance of success is theoretically smaller, the stimulus to work is greater. If there be fifty candidates for twelve posts, the amount of work done by each candidate tends to be greater than if there were only thirteen candidates for the same number of posts. There is, no doubt, a limit to the operation of this law. When the disproportion of candidates to places reaches a certain height, the smallness of the hope of success which the average candidate feels will diminish rather than stimulate his energy; but, in any case, the amount of work done will be vastly beyond the measure of the actual work which has an efficient value in determining success.

So with the trade competition in an ordinary commercial society. Though the amount of thrift which can be effectually exercised by the whole society is strictly limited, this limit imposes no such absolute restriction upon the thrift of any individual. The thrift of the individual consists in getting possession of the material forms of capital; whether or to what extent these forms are economically required, or will be actually and fully used to assist future production, is dependent on facts which are not immediately and clearly before the eyes of the individual when he is seeking to save.

It may be well here to call attention to an important fact which has a bearing upon the relation between the economically desirable rate of saving and the rate of consumption. The quantity of capital stored in Machinery and Plant at each stage in production required to assist a given rate of production of Commodities is by no means fixed. The constant tendency of improvements in the arts of manufacture, and even in the arts of storage of goods and retailing, is to lessen the amount of real Capital required at the different stages in production. Thus, assuming that the rate of consumption in a community remained the same, the amount of effectual saving which could be stored in forms of capital would continually diminish; that is to say, the present rate of production could be carried on with a smaller amount of Capital.

In Chapter II. we have proved—

That the existence of a distinct Quantitative Relation between the rate of Present Production and the rate of immediately Future Consumption implies a theoretic possibility of general Over-Supply (or Under-Demand).

We have now proved—

That the competition among individuals in an ordinary commercial society tends continually to the establishment of actual Over-Supply.

We have now to examine two considerations, which, according to most modern economists, furnish efficient checks to a condition of Over-Supply.

These are—

I. A fall in general prices, which, by causing an increased demand for Commodities, is alleged to provide an economic use for what would otherwise have been Over-Supply.

II. Such a fall in the rate of interest (or profit) as will act as a check upon Saving, and restore the proper relation between production and consumption.[1]

[1] So persistent is the assumption among economic writers that the machinery of commerce is a self-adjusting one which cannot get much out of working order, that they seldom take the trouble to distinctly state the nature of the economic checks to Over-Production. But the general tenour of their reasoning is in complete accord with the following statement of Läveleye :—'When there is a lack of equilibrium between production and consumption certain influences come into play, which tend to restore this in the following way :—Too many shoes are made. To sell the surplus shoemakers will lower their prices. This will have two results: First, the fall of price will increase the number of consumers; secondly, shoemakers, finding themselves at a loss, will make fewer shoes, until the equilibrium is here again established.' (Läveleye, 'Elements of Pol. Econ.,' p. 99.) This argument, irrefutable as applied to the interests of any single branch of production, is considered a sufficient answer to those who have asserted the possibility of general Over-Production.

Before passing to a closer examination of the value of these two checks, one point must be clearly marked. The fall in retail prices and the fall in rate of interest, which are the operative forces in these alleged checks, are both acknowledged to be results brought about by an actual condition of Over-Supply. However small this amount may be, there must be some Over-Supply actually existent before either of these alleged preventives can be set in motion. No mere tendency to Over-Supply can have any effect.[1] Much false argument in economics is based upon a wrong use of the term tendency. Loose thinkers are sometimes induced by their perception, that the main forces with which Economics deal are often checked or turned aside in practice, to speak of these forces as tendencies, meaning by the term forces which would act if they could. Now, such a tendency has no value and could have no effect; it has no real existence, and can work none of the miracles imputed to it. A force which does not act as it would otherwise have acted because its action is subject to the interference of another force does not therefore lapse into a tendency; it is just as real a force as before. There is no such thing as a tendency to Over-Supply. Either there is under supply of the forms of capital economically requisite to assist in producing what people would be willing to consume, or there is exactly the right number of forms, or there is Over-Supply. There is in no case any commercial

[1] Malthus clearly recognised that if a fall in profits was to serve as a relief to 'a glut of Commodities,' there must be an actual glut. See Malthus, 'Pol. Econ.,' Ch. I., s. III.

fact which answers to the name, 'tendency to Over-Supply.'

Let us now turn to the examination of the operation of the first of the two alleged preventive checks, that of falling prices.

The fuller statement of this economic argument is as follows .—The smallest quantity of general Over-Supply will cause a fall in general prices; this fall in general prices will increase the quantity of commodities demanded, and will continue to act in this manner until the quantity demanded has assumed the same relation to the increased Supply as the old quantity demanded bore to the old Supply.

So beautifully simple is this argument that economists who have thought it worth while to deal argumentatively with the theory of general Over-Supply have generally put it forward as the briefest and most complete refutation of a foolish heresy. Yet, when we come to a closer examination of this argument, the fallacy it rests upon will seem equally simple and palpable. In the first place, it might well be urged that the general Over-Supply may exist merely in the earlier stages of production; the excessive accumulation will most naturally at first take the shape of an excessive number of unfinished or finished goods, or of the machinery which operates at the early stages of production. In that case it would be possible to urge that, although the prices of unfinished or finished goods might fall owing to this excess, the prices of retail commodities might remain as before, the retailers reaping the whole advantage of the fall in wholesale prices.

It will, in fact, be shown later (*vide* Chapter VI.)

that this is what actually occurs in commercial communities; that the fall of wholesale prices is not immediately followed by a corresponding fall in retail prices; that the latter is slow of operation, and does not, when it occurs, exactly reflect the changes in wholesale prices.

But, in order that the fallacious nature of the main contention may be more apparent, we will not press this point here, but will assume that wherever the pressure of general Over-Supply may make itself felt the fall in prices which it brings about is straightway reflected in a corresponding fall of retail or shop prices. The simple question which is before us is this: Will the general fall of retail prices stimulate an increased demand for shop goods, and thus remedy the congestion due to over-production? If retail prices fall, it would seem as if purchasers ought to be able to purchase more than they did before, and that thus they will be tempted to raise their standard of living. But before a person makes a purchase he looks at two things: the price of the article and the condition of his purse. If he finds that he has less command of money than before, he may not be more able or more willing to increase his purchases, although the price of articles has fallen.

We have assumed a general fall in wholesale and retail prices. Before we can rightly ascertain whether this will serve to stimulate demand, we must ask another question. What is the effect of a general fall of prices on the Income of the Community? We are not here speaking of the real income of the Community, which is the sum of values created during the year, but of the money income of the Community.

We have seen that the money income[1] of each individual in an industrial community, whether received in the form of wage profit or rent, is ultimately paid out of the money received by retailers for the sale of commodities. If the amount of money received by retailers rises, the general money income of the community rises; and if the amount received by retailers falls, the general money income falls with it. Thus every rise and fall in retail prices (the money received by retailers) will mean a corresponding rise or fall of the money income of the community.[2] How, then, will a general decline of retail prices act as an effective stimulus to increased demand for Commodities, when the average income of consumers has fallen correspondingly? A man

[1] It is true that in commerce it is usual to include in a man's income not only the margin of profit upon sales effected, but also an estimated value of unsold goods, &c. But although it is convenient and reasonable that these should be taken into account in estimating the money income of the individual, they cannot rightly be considered in estimating the money income of the community, for if these unsold goods had been put into the market so as to force a sale, this sale could only have been effected by causing a still further reduction in general prices, and the total money received from the whole amount of sales would not have been greater than that from the smaller number.

[2] We are here assuming that a community is entirely composed of producers whose incomes are derived directly from sales of different kinds. It is, however, clear that people in receipt of fixed money incomes are enabled to raise their demand for commodities with every fall in retail prices. In so far, however, as certain individuals do not feel the effects of the general reduction of money incomes, others must feel it more severely. Thus, for example, if the mortgagee still gets his interest, the landlord suffers more severely in proportion.

who had previously an income of £.500 per annum will not be induced to raise his standard of living by a fall of fifty per cent. in retail prices when he perceives that his income has fallen to the level of £.250 a year.

There is one objection to the argument, which though it has been answered in effect by the proof that all incomes are derived from, and dependent on, retail sales, it may be well to deal with explicitly. The objection will take the following shape:—'Retail prices will only fall because the supply of Shop goods is greater than before, while the demand is supposed to remain the same. But the greater supply of Shop goods implies a larger number of sales effected at each preceding stage in the process of production. Now it is true that each of these sales has been effected at a lower price than previously, but it does not follow that the money income derived by makers and wholesale traders from their business is any less than before, for the increase in number of sales may be very well considered to compensate for the lower prices received. If, then, the money incomes of these men remain the same as before, or do not fall correspondingly with the fall of prices, when retail prices are touched they will be able to take advantage of the cheaper prices of shop goods, and will increase their demand.'

To this objection there is the following answer:— Along with the fall of retail prices will come a fall of the total receipts or incomes of all concerned in production. Assuming that up to the time when retail prices are affected, the incomes of makers and merchants were the same as before, immediately retail prices are affected the number of purchases from makers and merchants, even at the lower prices, is diminished, so that the latter find their incomes falling equally with the rate of fall of retail prices. The slightest decline in retail prices which has been supposed to induce those who up to the present moment have been in receipt of their usual money income, to increase their retail purchases, is found by them to equally affect their own incomes, so that though they would have increased their retail purchases had their income stood steady, they will not now attempt to do so. The real question at issue is one of time. If, when the maker and merchant learn that retail prices are falling, they look merely at their last month's receipts, they will say, 'Well, our income, though made out of more sales at lower prices, is steady; now that retail prices are falling we can afford to raise our standard of living.' But if, as is more probable, they look at the actual present and the probable future, they will see that with each fall in retail prices the demand for the goods they are selling is growing less, that orders are falling off, and wholesale prices falling still lower, and that their money income is actually shrinking in strict accord with the fall in retail prices. For it must be remembered that it takes no time for the effect of a fall in retail prices to operate along the whole process of production; immediately the receipts of retailers fall, the demands at each point in production fall correspondingly; the effects are, in effect, simultaneous. We can, therefore, assume no interval, even of a day, during which the maker or the merchant can feel justified by present considerations in increasing his demand for commodities.

But one final point remains for consideration. Suppose that the community, or any large proportion of the community, neglecting the corresponding shrinkage of their incomes, insisted on taking advantage of the fall in retail prices brought about by Over-Supply to increase their number of purchases of Commodities, what would be the result? Let us first note precisely the nature of the action we impute to them. Prices have fallen, say, twenty-five per cent., and all incomes have fallen twenty-five per cent., for we may assume for the purpose of argument that all incomes, whether received as wages, profit, or rent, are equally affected (though we shall see later on that this is not actually the case, and that we are only entitled to say that the average income has fallen twenty-five per cent.). Yet, notwithstanding the fact that they are no better off than before, we will assume that a considerable number of persons, looking only at the fall of prices, increase their demand for commodities without considering that by doing so they seem likely to cut down their normal rate of savings, or even to exceed their yearly income by running into debt. As they thus thoughtlessly and blindly increase their demand for commodities, they will find their money income rising with each increase of demand. For, in the first place, assuming the low retail prices were untouched by the increased demand, the number of retail sales has now increased, and with it the money incomes of retail traders; retail traders now increase their orders of wholesale goods, and once more, assuming the low prices stood, the income of wholesale merchants rises from the increased number of sales. In like manner, at every stage in production there is a rise of income through an increase of sales. But this is not the only way in which the reckless demand for Commodities raises incomes. As the fall of retail prices was caused by the growing excess of supply over quantity demanded at former prices, so the increased demand for commodities will raise retail prices again towards the old level. This old level will not, however, be reached until supply is once more brought into the normal, the old relation to quantity demanded; that is to say, until the whole of that Over-Supply of Shop goods, which was the immediate cause of the decline of prices, has been completely swallowed up. If we suppose that consumers insist on increasing their consumption of Commodities until this normal condition of prices has actually been restored, what will be their condition as regards money income and saving power? They will find their apparent recklessness to have the force of a well-founded faith. Their money income will rise apace with their increased consumption; the more they consume the more they will be able to consume. This will continue until they have consumed all that existed in the form of over-production and have restored prices to the normal level. If they do not stop even here, but, smitten with the desire for constantly improving their standard of comfort, continue to increase their demand beyond the former level, they will find that prices will rise, that money incomes will rise along with prices, and that production at every point will strain every nerve in order to keep pace with the increasing desire to consume, giving full economic employment to as much labour, capital, and natural agents as can be brought to bear upon the arts of production. Nor is this all. Having by an act of economic faith increased their consumption without regard to the virtue of thrift, they will find that along with every increase in consumption more thrift becomes feasible. For thrift is only operative when more forms of capital are economically required. So long as there existed Over-Supply there was no room for thrift, as this Over-Supply is removed by an increased rate of consumption, there is once more place for new forms of Capital, and thrift is again effectual. If the increased demand does not stop with the return to previous conditions, but continues to grow so as to strain the productive machine, there is an ever-growing use for more saving and more thrift. And not only is more thrift possible, but it is necessary.

If people would consume more they *must* save more; unless, indeed, their increased desire for consumption is a momentary freak, and has not the durability of a rational resolve. But *can* they save more? When people increase their consumption more saving may be required, but who will exercise it? The answer is a simple one. The people who are consuming more. And it is precisely because they are consuming more that they can save more. This is a paradox, but unlike most paradoxes which gain credence for a falsehood by tickling the ear with a pointed antithesis, it contains a truth which will bear the closest scrutiny. As the community can only increase its consumption by increasing its saving, it cannot increase its consumption without a proportionate increase to its saving fund. So long as there still exists any portion of Over-Supply, this increase of saving is not required, but the moment

Supply is once more brought to the normal relation with quantity demanded, any increase in the latter requires a corresponding increase in the former, and every increase in the former requires more Saving. But Saving is the result of the operation of motives on individuals. If people are bent on increasing as fast as possible their standard of consumption, how will they be induced to save more? In the following way. As they take advantage of the lower retail prices to increase their demand for Commodities, they will find that prices begin to rise; but they will also find that their money incomes are rising at a more rapid rate than the rise of prices, because it is not only affected proportionately by every rise of price, but also by the increased number of times the higher price is paid, that is by the increased number of sales. Thus, every individual will find that the money value of his income has risen, that he is able both to consume more and to save more. Of course it is open under such circumstances for any individual to use all his increased income as demand for commodities, and to save none of it; but he will pursue this course in the teeth of a constantly growing stimulus to save. Saving will be easier for him, because it can be effected not only without pinching, but along with an increasing rate of personal consumption, and it will be more advantageous for him, because it will be productive of the maximum of profit. For when increased consumption acts as a constant strain upon the productive aid of capital, it has been seen that each form of capital, each embodiment of saving, has a full economic value, and brings the maximum return of profit to its owner. If any considerable portion of the community still persist in neglecting the opportunity to save, and spend all their increased money incomes in demand for Commodities, they are thereby increasing the possibility of effective saving for others who are less extravagantly inclined, and will force the latter to save a larger proportion of their incomes by the incentive of a rise of profit, until the less extravagant are induced not only to do their own share of the necessary saving, but the share which the more extravagant refused to do.

It must, of course, always be borne in mind that so soon as all the labourers available for work are fully employed, or so soon as all the natural agents available for use are fully used, no further increase in consumption or in capital can take place. Since unused natural agents, whatever may be the case in the future, exist at present in practically unlimited quantities, we may exclude them from consideration. The limit to which we refer will be a limit to the aggregate of capital; in a given condition of the productive arts, each labourer can only efficiently co-operate with a certain maximum amount of capital; if there could be brought into existence more forms of capital than sufficed to furnish the maximum for every labourer, the surplus must be waste. So soon, therefore, as saving has accumulated this total, production will be limited by the aggregate of labour available for use. In this case consumption will be limited by production, and can only increase if the number of labourers increases, or if advances in the mechanical arts enable the existing number of labourers to effect the production of a larger quantity of wealth.

This is a correct account of what would happen if a whole community were to seize the opportunity of a general fall of retail prices, occasioned by Over-Supply, to increase the rate of consumption. It must, of course, be distinctly understood that if a single person, or a few persons alone in the community, raise their demand for commodities, they will not find their income rising with each increase in their consumption, nor will they find that they can save more as they spend more. The effect of their action will be spread over the whole community; so far as their increased consumption increases the general demand, it will operate in producing a slight rise in general prices, and in the incomes of all members of the community, but they themselves will reap no special benefit. It is only on the assumption that the community, as a whole, is incited to increase its consumption that the beneficial results above described will ensue. An individual who should thus increase his consumption while the rest of the community stood firm, would, no doubt, be conferring a slight public benefit, but, so far as his own interests were concerned, his act would be one of private extravagance.

It has been important to examine what would happen if the result of a fall of retail prices were an increase in the consumption of the community. But it has been seen that, paying regard to the ordinary motives that operate with men, there is no reason to hope that a fall of retail prices, which brought with it a corresponding fall in money incomes, would operate in this way.

Having shown that the first economic check which

is supposed to prevent any evil effects of over-production is entirely ineffectual, and tends rather to aggravate the evil, let us pass to the second check, which acts through the motive power of a fall in interest or profit.

It is alleged that a fall in the profit upon existing capital will remedy the evil of Under-Demand by restoring the proper economic relations between Production and Consumption. If people find that they cannot get the usual return for the use of their savings, they will not save so much, it is urged.

Now, if a fall of Profit is to induce people to save less, it must operate in one of two ways, either by inducing them to spend more or by inducing them to produce less.

First, let us ask, will a fall in Profit increase the amount of Consumption? Let us assume, for purposes of convenience, that there is an even fall in all profits. How will this fact cause increased consumption? Will the Capitalist consume more? A fall in profit means to him a fall in income, and it is absurd to suppose that he will be induced to increase his expenditure in the teeth of a falling income. The knowledge that he can get a smaller return than before for the same exertion of thrift will not induce him to put on an extra carriage and increase his household expenses when his books show a declining income. Will the working-classes consume more? Supporters of Mr. Mill's wage-fund theory would, no doubt, reply in the affirmative; each fall in profit means to them a rise in wages, and they might reasonably urge that the working-classes would spend their increased income in raising their standard of living; that is, in increasing the aggregate of Consumption. But the fallacy of the wages-fund has been already sufficiently exposed. There is no ground for assuming that a fall in profit implies a rise in wages; on the contrary, it has been seen that a fall in profit caused by the existence of excessive capital is only one aspect of a larger phenomenon. It was seen that Under-consumption, acting through the agency of Over-supply, reduced not the income of one class of producers, but the fund from which all incomes were paid at each point in the line of production; that is to say, the aggregate income of the community was reduced. We cannot suppose that when the average rate of incomes is falling, individuals will be induced to increase their rate of consumption by the fact that the premium upon thrift is correspondingly diminished.

Since a fall in profit cannot reasonably be expected to operate by increasing consumption, we are obliged to look for its effect in diminishing production. It is so far from being our intention to deny that a fall of profit, due to Over-Supply, will check production, that the admission of the operation of this check forms the very centre of our argument. We shall show in the succeeding chapters how this check upon production does not imply a diminution in the use of the forms of capital and labour, but a wasteful use of these same forms due to a derangement of the proper economic relations between the amounts of capital and labour, functioning at different points in the industrial machine. In the diminished production which is here adduced, as the result of this economic check of a fall of profit, we shall see the most pernicious form of the disease called Depression in Trade.

To sum up the results arrived at in this chapter, we have seen that though the community can have no interest in creating a condition of general Over-supply or Under-consumption, the result may be brought about by the conflicting interests of individuals, because, though there is a strict limit to the amount of saving which a community may do in a given state of general demand, there is no such limit to the saving power of the individual. We have examined the two economic checks which are alleged to be efficient preventives of any evil results which might arise from an excessive rate of production. It has been seen that an actual condition of Over-production must exist before either of these economic forces can be set in operation. The first force, that of a general fall of prices, we have proved can have no power to restore a right relation between production and consumption. The second force, that of falling profit, is seen to operate by acting as a check upon production, and can only act by thus lowering the source of all incomes. The fall of average income thus brought about has been already identified with the phenomena called Depression of Trade. It is, therefore, clear that the self-acting checks on which Political Economy has hitherto relied to prevent any evil results which might arise from an increase of production without a corresponding increase of consumption, are unable to achieve this end. The one check, that of falling prices, is entirely inoperative; the other, that of falling profit, is the immediate cause of the very malady which it is supposed to prevent.

CHAPTER V.

EXPANSION AND CONTRACTION OF TRADE.

IN economics, where we are shut off from the possibility of strictly scientific experiment, there are only two ways of appealing to experience in attestation of the validity of an argument. We may appeal to statistics, and by careful collection, selection, and application support and illustrate the truth we wish to impress; but the path of statistical inquiry is a slippery one, and we are frequently confronted with the fact of two equally competent authorities with the same figures at their disposal arriving at totally different conclusions. The other way is to take an extreme case, where the force or phenomenon whose operation we are investigating assumes a quite abnormal importance. History, even the history of trade, sometimes affords us a striking example which serves to bring out in dramatic proportion the true bearings of a case, and, carefully treated, throws clearer light upon the subject than the largest and most reliable array of statistical facts.

In the previous chapters we have shown how an

increase or a decrease in consumption acted respectively as a stimulus or a check to Production, and we related the phenomenon of Depression in Trade to the phenomenon of Under-Consumption as manifested in the attempt of the community to save a larger proportion of its income than was required to furnish the capital necessary to maintain the desired rate of production. It is now our object to illustrate from the period of the Franco-German war the operation of a sudden large increase in consumption followed by a sudden return to a normal condition of consumption.

From an economic point of view the Franco-German war may be regarded as a sudden and enormous increase of consumption or quantity of commodities demanded combined with a sudden and enormous withdrawal of the Requisites of Production from use. Not merely were the belligerent states purchasers of large quantities of all kinds of produce, such as food, clothing, vehicles, guns, ammunition, and all the apparatus of war, but the mills, machinery, and other plant in these states were compelled to stand wholly or partially idle by reason of the abstraction of the labourers to serve as soldiers.

Now, the first effect of this enormous new Demand of the belligerent Governments which we have to note, has relation to Saving. It has been shown that Saving is only effective in proportion as there is a present demand for the use of the wealth which is saved. To save is to create a lien or claim upon future production, and one method of effecting this purpose is by giving up existing commodities to others to consume in the present, subject to the condition that these 'others' shall at any desired future time return to the lender an equivalent of newly-created wealth. The more, therefore, that others, able to give effective liens on the future, are willing to consume in the present, the more the liens that can be established on the future, that is, the more saving. When a thrifty saving folk can find a responsible Government ready to accept enormous quantities of beef, butter, shoes, coats, &c., and to promise to provide the owners of them with dinners, clothing, &c., through all future time, they are willing to provide these commodities. The method by which this Saving is effected is briefly this: The thrifty saving folk habitually pay the money they save into the banks; these banks, either directly or through other bankers, hand over this money to the belligerent powers in the shape of a loan; the latter immediately pass on the money to traders and received commodities in return. The commodities thus received represent the 'Saving' which was able to be effected because of the increased demand for commodities exerted by the belligerent Governments. The commodities which had been paid in to the community's 'Stock' against the 'purchasing power' paid to the saving folk were received by the belligerent powers, and the liens or debts created by these powers were received by the saving folk. Under these circumstances no Over-Supply could possibly accumulate. Some individual or other possesses the power to purchase every commodity that is offered for sale; if he does not wish to use that power he will wish to save and accumulate it; in this case he hands it over in a money shape to the banks which are furnishing purchasing power to the belligerent states; these states exercise all the purchasing power they can get hold of as a demand for commodities. Thus, no over-supply could possibly exist, for whether individual producers wished to consume or to save, the commodities were equally demanded for consumption. Since the demand for commodities must always suffice to induce their replacement by new products, and since there is no limit to the quantity demanded, there is likewise no limit to the amount of production other than the limit imposed by the Requisites of Production themselves. No matter how much was produced, no fall in price could occur, for the quantity demanded was of necessity always the utmost that could be supplied.

It is next important to note the results of this rise in quantity demanded and the stimulus it gave to production, upon the gain of those engaged in productive work.

How does this desire on the part of consumers to consume as much as can possibly be produced affect profits? In answering this question we have to use for the first time the broad distinction between the two classes of producers, the makers (producers in the narrow loose sense) and the traders. What proportion of the total value of the commodity will fall to the maker, and what to the trader in the case of this enlarged demand? It is clear that everything the maker can make he can find a trader to buy at the current price, and everything that a trader holds he can find a consumer to buy at the current price. It might, therefore, appear at first sight that neither maker nor trader possessed any advantage over the other. But is this so? The maker can sell all he makes, the amount each particular maker sells is only limited by the absolute limits of his power to shape material; he is in no wise affected by the competition of other makers, who can all likewise sell everything they can make. But with the trader it is different; he, too, can sell all that he can get hold of, but the amount he can get hold of is not absolutely limited save by the total amount which is produced; each trader is able to dispose of as large a proportion of this total as he can get into his own hands; but this amount is limited by the desire of every other trader to do the same. Thus, while the maker in effecting sales is not hampered by the competition of other makers, the trader is hampered by the continual competition of other traders seeking to sell as large a share as possible of the increased production to consumers. Traders will thus outbid one another in purchasing from makers, raising their offers to the point which leaves to them the barest margin of profit for which they are willing to continue their work. Paying higher prices to makers, it might appear that they would be able to recoup themselves by raising the prices to consumers. But if they succeed in raising the prices to consumers they will still be unable to keep a larger profit for themselves, for the competition by which each will seek to effect as many sales as possible will oblige them to offer increased prices to makers, who would thus reap the whole advantage of the rise. It is this power of makers to secure for themselves the whole value of the commodity, minus the least fraction for which traders are willing to conduct their trade, at all times when the quantity of commodities demanded is the utmost that can be supplied, that accounts for the rise of wholesale prices and of makers' profits which occurred in the years 1871, 1872, 1873. The traders wished to buy more goods than makers could supply, and the only limit to the inter-competition of traders was their refusal to give makers more than the price they would receive from consumers. The maker could, in effect, say, 'The retail price of this commodity is so much; I will allow you a bare minimum of profit and no more; if you are not content with that, your neighbour will be.' The trader had no alternative, he must content himself with this minimum of profit, or receive nothing. Makers, under these circumstances, received within a fraction of the whole value produced, that is to say, the money they received would when exchanged by them for 'subsistence conveniences and amusement' buy back the full equivalent of the commodities produced, minus the traders' least profit. Under these circumstances all available capital and labour engaged itself in making, all traders who were able became makers, or added a 'making' department to their trading house. The number of traders tended to fall to the minimum required for the work of effectively distributing goods, and the productive powers of the community were taxed to the utmost. Never was there a period of such marked activity in production, initiated by the vast increase in expenditure of the belligerent powers. This extreme activity was plainly visible in every commercial country which had direct or indirect trade relations with France or Germany. For example, it is indisputable that the immense prosperity enjoyed by English producers during the Franco-German war, and for some time afterwards, must be attributed directly to the prodigious waste of wealth which that war occasioned. The full extent of what was meant by the demand for commodities involved in this unproductive expenditure of war should be clearly realised. This increased demand for commodities was not merely a demand that a larger amount of raw material should be turned into food, guns, saddles, clothes, &c., for consumption; it was also a demand which was effective in calling into existence new and immense quantities of machinery and plant required to assist in the work of increased production of commodities. This latter fact has an important special significance, for it serves to explain how it was that the wonderful activity in trade did not collapse as soon as the abnormal demand for commodities was remitted, that is at the close of the war. A large part of the saving stimulated by the increased war demand found a natural investment in the construction of machinery and plant to assist production and in other machinery and plant to assist the production of the first machinery, and so forth. The enormous quantity of new plant which stood in France and other European countries at the close of 1873 represented actual savings that had been effected during the years immediately subsequent to this great war. The huge war debt incurred by France, and paid in the next few years, extended her war expenditure considerably beyond the actual period of the war, and provided a combined use for the saving and the mass of forms of capital in which it had been stored.

But even when the abnormal consumption engendered by the war declined, the full effects were not felt at once, or suddenly. Even after the Government had ceased to demand war supplies, and to create debts which furnished investments for the savings of the thrifty, and provided work for the enormous increase of plant, the full-blown phenomenon of Over-Supply was not visible at once. The plant and machinery in process of construction was advanced step by step towards completion, although its use was no longer wanted, for speculators had not realised the glut they were creating. The impetus of saving still continued; when no investments of the old order were feasible, there sprang up a series of bubble companies which offered bogus investments and swallowed up and consumed the savings of the unwary just as effectually as had the war expenditure, save that the paper they left in the hands of investors was waste-paper instead of representing sound liens upon future production. An examination of a few of the prospectuses of the companies actually floated in 1872 and 1873 justifies the assumption that at a period when such concerns could find promoters and investors, there can have been no opening for investment in any sort of Plant or Stock required to supply the current consumption.

We have now passed through an industrial phase, in which an abnormal consumption aroused the full productive powers of the community, provided the fullest employment for all capital and labour, and stimulated the creation of wealth to the utmost extent. We proceed to examine the further phase, when this extraordinary consumption had ceased, and the amount of capital, the rate of production, and the rate of saving were all in excess of what was economically required to supply the amount of commodities the community[1] was content to consume. In order to clearly understand what happened, it is best to look first at the money aspect of the case. For although, if we consider the community as a whole, natural agents, capital and labour, are the requisites of production, if we consider the individual, money is the only requisite. With money he can procure the use of plant and labour, and can produce what commodity he likes; without money he can do nothing. Now, look at the period of the Franco-German war and the years following from the point of view of the capitalist manufacturer. So long as the demand for commodities continued, money had been constantly and rapidly returned to capitalist makers in the ordinary process of trade. The portion of the income (money) of the community spent by each member in the purchase of 'utilities and conveniences' was returned into the hands of 'makers' as a demand for the replacement of retailing stock, the portion of the income that was 'saved' passed into the makers' hands by the intervention of the lien-creating government as payment for the materials of war or other commodities whose consumption increased the aggregate of the quantity demanded, and when these demands had ceased,

[1] We have used the term community because the industrial community of the world is one, and the effects here described were felt in a more or less degree by all European countries and the United States.

it still reached capitalist makers' hands as demand for the new forms of capital, *i.e.*, machinery, ships, railways, &c., which, owing to the abnormal war demand, had appeared to be necessary. Thus all the money distributed by capitalist makers as Demand for the Use of Requisites of Production (*i.e.*, wages, rent, profits) was constantly returned to them as demand for more goods. This lasted so long as the extra consumption strained to the utmost the productive powers of the community. But when the relaxed consumption began to exhibit a glut of the different forms of capital, and saving individuals began to refuse to invest their savings directly in any scheme that could be suggested, but preferred to retain the savings in their own hands, the capitalist maker no longer received sufficient money to continue their demand for the use of the requisites of production at the old rate. Individuals no longer embarked their savings on their own account in the work of aiding production, but paid them in to banks. At first no very obvious change ensued. Though capitalist makers no longer received the money in the ordinary course of trade, they could obtain what they wanted from bankers. Thus for some little time, so long as they could offer to the banks what seemed fair security for repayment, they could obtain the money requisite to maintain the current rate of production. But when, owing to the reduction in quantity demanded, they were unable to maintain their previous rate of sales, their stock of goods accumulated in the warehouses constantly grew, while at the same time their liabilities to the banks grew correspondingly. Sooner or later a crisis was inevitable. The moment bankers refused to continue increasing their loans to capitalist makers and speculators, and, on the contrary, pressed for repayment of their advances, the holders of this surplus stock of goods were forced to sell at any price they could get in order to escape or postpone bankruptcy. Traders, finding that any price they chose to offer was accepted, rapidly lowered their offers. The fall in wholesale prices thus begun continued until the profit of makers fell so low that a sufficient number refused to continue making, and by ceasing to make restored the equation between production and consumption. This process of economic adjustment between the rate of Production and Consumption is, of course, extremely slow, and while it is going on all those phenomena which indicate Depression in Trade are exceptionally visible.

First, we have to note a complete reversal of the previous apportionment of profits. We saw that while the special demand occasioned by the war operated, the productive work of makers was rewarded by the whole of the commodities produced, with the exception of that minimum which sufficed to induce traders to continue their work of distribution. Now that demand is relaxed, and more is being produced than is required to supply the current rate of consumption, the case is very different. Formerly every maker could sell all he made, and no competition of his fellow-makers brought down his prices. Now makers wish to sell more than traders are willing to buy; every trader can easily buy as much as he wants at current prices, while every trader is competing with his fellows to sell as many of his goods as possible. The limit is no longer the rate of possible production, but the rate of consumption. This gives to the traders an advantage precisely equivalent to that which makers formerly possessed. Wholesale prices fall until they barely cover the cost of production, reducing the profits of makers to the minimum for which they will consent to continue producing, or, more strictly speaking, the former rate of profit is turned into such a rate of loss as will gradually operate in driving a sufficient number of makers from the work of making. Just as the maker was formerly able to reduce the trader's profit to a minimum, so now the trader is able to say to the maker: 'I will pay you for your goods the bare cost of production; if you do not care to take it, I can find other makers who will.' The maker has no alternative, for he has got goods which he does not want, and their price, money, is essential to enable him to meet his current expenses. If he does not accept the trader's offer he knows that other makers, still more in need of money, will do so.

Thus it appears that one speedy result of such a decline of wholesale prices as results from a relaxed demand is the elevation of traders' profits. It is true that a fall in retail prices will eventually follow the fall in wholesale prices, but it will subsequently be shown that this operation is a slow one. Meanwhile we have a period in which traders reap immense profits. It is well known that in the period from 1873 onward, while makers were being ruined on all sides, merchants and retail tradesmen were making large fortunes.

It has already been proved that the whole value of the commodity produced is returned in the form of profit, wages, and rent, to those who have assisted in producing it. Taking the largest division of producers, makers and traders, we are now able to lay down the following law with regard to the portion of the commodity which falls to the two classes respectively:—'When the rate of consumption gives full employment to the existing requisites of production, the makers get the whole value of the commodity, less the minimum for which traders will consent to continue trade. When the rate of consumption fails to give full employment to the existing requisites of production, the traders get the whole value of the commodity, less the minimum for which makers will consent to continue making.' This conclusion must be borne in mind when the fuller investigation of the effects of an industrial crisis on the various classes of producers is opened.

The rise in traders' profits and the fall in makers' profits will naturally result in a gradual withdrawal of capital and labour from making and its application to trading. Much capital and labour cannot be so withdrawn, but new savings seeking an investment and fresh labour entering the market will employ itself in the more profitable form of trading, and as much of the old capital and labour as can be withdrawn will be applied to trading. Now, in connection with this increase in the number of traders, there are two important points to notice.

First. It might appear as if the increased competition thus introduced among retailers ought to operate in rapidly reducing the retail prices to correspond with the reduction of wholesale prices. But the fact that retail prices do not, in fact, seem to respond to variations in wholesale prices has been noticed by Mill, who also incidentally assigns the true cause. "Retail price, the price paid by the actual consumer, seems to feel very slowly and imperfectly the effects of competition, and when competition does exist, it often, instead of lowering the prices, *merely divides the gains of the high price among a greater number of sellers*. Hence it is that of the price paid by the consumer so large a proportion is absorbed by the gains of retailers, and anyone who inquires into the amount which reaches the hands of those who made the things he buys will often be astonished at its smallness." (Mill, II., Ch. IV., s. 3.)

As soon as the retailing ranks are swelled by deserters from manufacture, and by the addition of new-born labour, instead of a large and rapid reduction in retail prices, the old prices are for the most part maintained, each trader doing, on the average, a smaller business than before. It is not here maintained that no fall in retail prices eventually occurs, but only that the fall is slow in operating, and when it does come does not correspond in extent to the fall in wholesale prices. The same cause which frequently induces fishmongers and fruiterers to destroy a portion of their stock in preference to selling it at reduced prices operates in regard to the whole of retail trade. Traders will prefer to do a smaller business, gaining a higher profit on each sale, than by successful competition with their fellows to do a larger business, with lower profits on each sale. But these reasons, while they may serve to explain why the fall of retail prices is slow to follow the fall in wholesale prices, do not furnish a sufficient explanation of the fact that retail prices do not eventually fall in a corresponding degree with wholesale prices.

That wholesale prices fluctuate much more suddenly and violently than retail prices is a well-recognised industrial fact. Moreover, not only are those fluctuations more rapid, but they represent a much larger divergence from average prices.

The reasons for this comparative want of flexibility in retail prices reside in the detailed conditions of retail trade. If the average consumer had as intimate a knowledge of all the details affecting the prices of every kind of commodity he buys, as the trader has of the special goods he buys from makers; if he were as keen in ascertaining and taking full advantage of the slightest fall of price; if he were absolutely independent of locality; and, most important of all, if he were able to fully seize the opportunity of a fall in prices to lay in a large stock of commodities, we might have the same rapid and large fluctuations in retail prices as in wholesale. But competition among retailers is, in a large measure, confined by locality, and even in that locality a slight rise or fall of any tradesman's prices will but slightly affect the bulk of his trade, because his customers do not compare prices, even inside the limited radius, as carefully as tradesmen do the prices of makers. But while the consumer suffers from ignorance of prices, he suffers still more from incapacity to recognise differences of quality in goods. While he gives some attention, at least, to rises and falls of price, as a rule he is extremely slow to recognise the most marked changes in quality. If a tradesman, instead of raising his prices, substitutes inferior articles for what he sold formerly, he can raise his profits without running much risk of losing his custom. In short, the trader is a specialist with regard to the prices and qualities of the things he buys from makers; the consumer, who buys not one but every kind of thing from traders, is not a specialist, and suffers accordingly. The tradesman knows that if he lowered his prices to the full extent which a fall in wholesale prices would justify him in doing, he would not thereby be enabled to get hold of all the trade of his neighbours as would be the case in an ideal state of competition. He recognises, on the contrary, that such a fall of prices would not bring an increase in custom sufficient to increase the profits of his business. Hence, the tradesman never lowers his price more than the comparatively slight competition of surrounding tradesmen obliges him to do. When a fall in wholesale prices has thus raised the profits of retail trade, is the tradesman able to retain his superior position? No; the higher gains of retail trade, as has been said, attract fresh capital and labour into that branch of production. A retail business can be started more quickly, with less capital, and with less knowledge, as a rule, than a wholesale or manufacturing business. Hence it arises that while existing makers reap the full advantage of a rise of profits so long as quantity demanded equals the utmost that can be supplied, any rise of retail profits is quickly checked by a rapid increase of that limited form of competition which acts upon retailers.

This rapid and easy increase of retailers operates in this way: the newcomers establishing themselves in convenient localities, not too close to their competitors, take the current prices and try to make a custom for themselves out of the customers of their neighbours, not trusting so much to the inducement of lower prices as to other attractions and conveniences of neighbourhood, affability, shop front, advertisements, &c. Hence it arises that, instead of lowering retail prices, the competition engendered by high retail gains 'merely divides the gains of the high price among a greater number of sellers.'

That the retail vendor of commodities has generally a distinct advantage in knowledge over his customers, and that the ordinary process of barter and competition cannot be relied upon to determine prices, is generally acknowledged. It is, indeed, this truth which furnishes the reasonable basis of much modern legislation. Even the strictest of the orthodox economists would hesitate to pose as an advocate of unrestricted competition in cab fares.

It is at once recognised that the purchaser is, owing to the smallness of the purchase, to lack of time, and to ignorance of important details, quite unable to hold his own with the seller, and the State steps in and protects him by special regulations. Similarly, it has been found that purchasers, even when poor, and with every inducement to see that they get 'their money's worth,' are not merely unable to judge of quality, but even of so simple a matter as quantity; and the law has, in order to prevent grave abuses of the power which the retailer possesses, to order that retailers of coal, bread, &c.

should sell by weight, and appoints inspectors to see that this is actually done, and enforces penalties against those who fail to observe the regulations. Against fraudulent descriptions of goods we have similarly a list of enactments dealing with such articles as milk, butter, meat, fish, vegetables, and the like, the *raison d'être* of these Acts being that the purchaser is not merely unable to judge whether the article supplied to him is what it professes to be, but even whether it is fit for human food. If, however, it is admitted that the purchaser does not know what he is buying from the retailer, and cannot in many cases even determine the quantity that he gets, it is obvious that the law of competition no longer applies. The purchaser can only estimate the quality of goods by the price, and if a retailer lowers his prices, his customers assume immediately that the quality is proportionately lower. In small grocers' shops it is habitual to get two or three qualities of butter out of a single tub, and the purchasers of the higher-priced butter never for a moment suspect that the lower-priced is identical in every respect. The fact that regulations of the character noticed above have been passed by a representative Parliament, and have hardly been resisted even by the most determined upholders of free competition, points irresistibly to the conclusion that, in the opinion of the mass of the community, the purchaser is not on terms of equality with the retailer, and it necessarily follows that no free competition can take place. Where, however, prices are not determined by competition, custom is usually the determinant. In retail prices, therefore, custom reigns almost supreme, merely modified by the slow and partial effects of competition at such points and to such extent as the purchaser learns something of the real value of the articles he buys.

The existence of co-operative societies, the fact that wholesale dealers are also purchasers at retail prices, and similar causes, slowly and imperceptibly leaven the great mass of purchasers, and a corresponding adjustment of retail and wholesale prices tends to be produced, provided, of course, that no further variation in wholesale price again upsets the adjustment, and leaves the slow process to be again repeated.

To the same cause, custom, we may ascribe the fact that when wholesale prices are rising the retailer is unable to raise his price to a corresponding degree. For while the consumer is not induced to change his grocer or his tailor, from the fact that A. and B., another grocer and another tailor, have reduced their prices, because he is apt to attribute the conduct of the latter to a lowering in the quality of their goods, yet if his grocer or his tailor raise their prices while the prices of A. and B. remain unchanged, he will at once be apt to consider that his grocer and tailor are outrageous in their charges, and will forthwith transfer his custom to A. and B. Hence we get the curious conclusion that if a tradesman lowers his price twenty per cent. he will not compensate his loss by the increase of his sales, but if he raises his price twenty per cent. his gain on each sale will be more than compensated by a falling-off in sales The average consumer living, as he considers, just within his income, is more affected by a rise of price than by a fall. A fall of prices will not readily induce him to raise his standard of living to a corresponding extent;

a rise of prices, on the other hand, will act as an almost immediate check. When men who are in the habit of spending a certain number of pounds a-year find a sudden considerable rise in general prices, they are ready and believe themselves compelled to reduce the aggregate of their purchases.[1]

[1] The fact that retail prices are not wholly competition prices, and do not fluctuate with every fluctuation in the wholesale market, has been universally recognised by economists. The following quotations will serve to illustrate the fact of this recognition. It should, however, be observed that economists, one and all, have failed signally to recognise the important economic results which attend this want of correspondence in the movement of wholesale and retail prices. The critical importance of this will be manifested in the subsequent development of our argument.

"On one side is the merchant, who, by frequent resort to the wholesale dealer, is kept advised of the conditions of the market. On the other side is the 'customer,' a creature of custom, as the term implies; often ignorant, in the widest sense of the word, unintelligent, and untrained; always and necessarily ignorant in the special sense of being unacquainted with the conditions which should determine price, not knowing what a commodity ought to cost, and in the case of many classes of commodities, unable to judge of the quality of the goods offered; perhaps at the mercy of the dealer in the matter of the measure or weight. The merchant, again, is the possessor of capital, and can wait to dispose of his goods at the best time. The customer, on the other hand, is generally in urgent need of commodities for immediate use, and frequently poor, so that he must buy in small quantities; perhaps even in debt, so that he feels under a strong constraint to trade only with his creditor, who thus holds him at a double disadvantage, for how can he quarrel, as to quality, measure, or price, with the man whom he is not able to pay for goods already had and consumed?" (Mr. F. A. Walker, 'Pol. Ec.,' 3rd ed., pp. 108, 109.)

"The transactions" (retail) "do not take place between dealers possessing, or with opportunities of acquiring, equal knowledge respecting the commodities dealt in, but between experts on one side, and on the other, persons in most cases wholly ignorant of the circumstances at the time affecting the market. Between persons

Second. It has been seen that the result of the collapse of wholesale prices which followed the commer-

so qualified the game of exchange, if the rules be rigorously enforced, is not a fair one; and it has consequently been recognised, universally in England, and very extensively among the better class of retail dealers in continental countries, as a principle of commercial morality, that the dealer should not demand from his customer a higher price for his commodity than the lowest he is prepared to take." (Prof. Cairnes, 'Some Leading Principles Pol. Ec.,' pp. 113, 114.)

"Retail prices fluctuate less than wholesale prices. The reason of this is that the retailer can keep his customers if he satisfies them that on the whole his prices are fair. They do not watch the market closely; they do not know whether in each separate charge he has made proper allowance for the fluctuations of the market. But in large wholesale transactions the purchaser examines each bargain on its own merits. In important transactions the higgling and bargaining of the market are a fit occupation for business men; but in most retail transactions it is a waste of time and energy to bargain." (Prof. Marshall, 'Economics of Industry,' Book III., Chap. III., s. 9.)

"Suppose that the services of any particular class of labourers receive, on the average, a disproportionately high remuneration as compared with those of other classes; there are two ways in which this excess can be reduced; either—

"(1) By lowering the price of a given quantity of the utilities produced by the workers in question; or

"(2) By increasing the number of persons competing to produce such utilities, without augmenting their aggregate produce, owing to the increased difficulty that each has in finding customers.

"So far as this latter takes place, the effect of competition on production is positively disadvantageous.

"In actual experience this effect seems to occur most conspicuously in the case of services of which the purchasers are somewhat deficient in commercial keenness and activity; so that each producer thinks himself likely to gain more, on the whole, by keeping up the price of his services, rather than by lowering it to attract custom.

"An example of this kind is furnished by retail trade, especially the retail trade of the smaller shops to which the poorer classes chiefly resort; since the remarkable success of the co-operative cial crisis of 1873, due to the cessation of the creation of new plant and raw material, induced by the abnormal war consumption, was a large and rapid increase of the retailing class. When production was stimulated to the utmost, and when everything that was produced readily found consumers, the retailing class was kept down to the narrowest limit sufficient to distribute what was made. Now that consumption has diminished and more can be produced than can find a market, makers have become retailers, and the number of retailers relatively to makers has considerably increased. The point of importance is to notice the effect which this change has brought about upon the total of the commodities created, and its relation to the use of requisites of production stored in them. When demand was pulling tight the reins of production, and capital and labour were strained to the utmost endeavour, each form of capital and every labourer found a full economic use stored in the form of wealth which went to satisfy the large demand. When the decline in demand slackened the reins of production, a large amount of the capital and labour engaged at each point in the productive machinery became superfluous. This superfluity of

stores of artizans implies a considerable waste of shopkeepers' time and labour under the system previously universal.

. . . . .

"But, again, the importance to each individual of finding purchasers for his commodity also leads to a further waste, socially speaking, in the expenditure incurred for the sole purpose of attaining this result.

"A large part of the cost of advertisements, of agents and 'travellers,' of attractive shop-fronts, &c., come under this head." (Sidgwick, 'Prin. Pol. Ec.,' Book III., Chap. II., pp. 416, 417.)

the requisites of production was first manifested in the closure of some mills and factories, in the half-time or irregular working of others, and in a general slackening of the activity of those engaged in making. The same effect was not, however, visible in Retailing. It is true that as many goods did not pass through the hands of each retailer as before, when there was more retailing to be done, while, on the other hand, the number of retailers was constantly growing by fresh accessions from the ranks of makers who had failed, or were attracted by the apparent prosperity of retailers. Yet all this increased body of retailers appeared to be busy. The less retailing there was for each one to do, the keener the competition to do as much as possible. Where there was one retailer before to do a given quantity of retailing, there were now two. The two were just as busy, worked just as hard as the one formerly, the extra labour being swallowed up in the work of competing. This was the era of touting and advertising. There were more merchants, more agents, more shops, more shopmen in each shop, all strenuously exerting themselves to secure the same quantity of trade formerly conducted by a smaller quantity of labour. So, too, the plant of every kind engaged in assisting this trade was greater than before. It is not, indeed, fair to describe this increase of retailing work as absolutely wasted. In so far as the extra advertising and touting assists not to deceive and swindle consumers, but to enable them to learn more precisely what they want and where to get it; in so far as the more numerous shops and shopmen enable them more quickly and easily to satisfy these wants, the extra labour must be considered to perform a service which has distinct value as a commodity. If there are two attendants in a shop it is obvious that customers can be more quickly and efficiently served than if there is only one; if there are four the service will be better than if there were two; if there were eight, better still, and so on. But it is equally clear that when a certain limit of number is reached, each additional hand is of less and less value, and that as you increase the number you approach nearer to a point where any additional work would only have a nominal value. Or, again, if you have two grocers' shops in a particular street competing for the surrounding customers, the wants of the neighbourhood will be adequately supplied; if two more grocers open shops in the same street, dividing the custom with the two previous ones, the advantage to the neighbourhood will be extremely small; in fact, it might be said that the capital and labour of two of the four establishments was wasted. Look at it from the point of view of labour, for that of capital is less important. In making an article it is not economically possible that more than a certain amount of labour should be used; in every order for goods that is executed the manufacturer takes care that the minimum of labour shall be employed. But when articles are turned out of the factory they are not fully produced commodities; the productive work of making has to be supplemented by the productive work of trading. Now, it appears that while there is a limit to the amount of labour expended in making a certain quantity of goods, there is no such limit to the labour expended in advancing these goods to the position of commodities, and placing them in a finished state in the hands of consumers. Now, let us compare the average productiveness of labour when a high rate of consumption stimulates making and keeps the number of retailers at a minimum, with the condition brought about when a relaxed demand has increased the number of retailers at the expense of makers. In the former condition each commodity placed in the hands of a consumer had packed into it the smallest quantity of Uses of Requisites of Production that was possible, the productive energy of the community was taxed to the utmost, and the most rigid economy of labour was practised. But in the other case it is quite different. Each commodity had the same amount of making energy packed into it, but the amount of retailing work contained in it and paid for in the price was much greater than before. Looking at it from the point of view of the worker, it may be said that, assuming the retailing class to be already adequate to distribute with fair regularity and speed the goods that are made, every worker who is driven out of the making business into the retailing business is driven from a more productive to a less productive Use of his labour. What holds of labour holds to a less extent of capital and natural agents. The comparatively useless stores and shops, &c., represent a comparative waste of capital and land. Thus, it may be concluded that when a high rate of consumption keeps tense the productive energies of the nation, there is packed in each commodity the minimum of Use of each of the Requisites of Production, and that when the rate of production tends to exceed the rate of consumption, there is the maximum of use of each of these Requisites of Production in each commodity. But it has been admitted that each commodity ultimately furnishes the payment for the use of the Requisites of Production it contains; that is to say, that out of each commodity is paid the wages, profits, rent of all those who have assisted in producing it. It follows that where each commodity contains a large amount of the Uses of Requisites of Production, the scale of payment is proportionately small. Labour, capital, land, are more valuable and get larger return for their use when the smallest amount of that use suffices to assist the production of a commodity. In other terms, the same amount of labour, capital, land, produces a greater quantity of commodities when the rate of consumption is on a level with the greatest possible rate of production, a smaller quantity of commodities when the rate of consumption is below that of possible production. In short, wages, profits, rent are high when consumption is high relatively to what could be produced, low when consumption is low relatively to what could be produced. Whether the several Requisites of Production gain equally by a rise in consumption relative to production; or if not, what laws regulate the difference in their respective gains, are questions which receive a separate investigation in the next chapter.

By using as an illustration an abnormal period of industrial history we have endeavoured to show how a large increase in quantity demanded or consumption operated in providing a full use for all the superfluous capital which tended to congest the industrial body, in stimulating to the utmost the productive powers of the community, calling forth increased creation of wealth and providing a use for it, and paying the highest prices in the form of wages, profits, rent to the owners of Requisites of Production. We have also shown how, when the demand collapsed, and the rate of consumption relatively to production fell, a commercial crisis followed, causing a great dislocation of trade, forms of capital being wasted, and labour thrown out of employment; that afterwards there was a gradual drifting of labour into retailing, which swelled abnormally the number of traders, issuing in a condition of depressed trade, wherein a smaller quantity of commodities came to be divided as payment of wages, profits, rents, making a general fall of income in the community.

To make the importance of this argument clearer let us assume that in a healthy state of commerce 9-10ths of an article go to the makers and 1-10th to the retailer; we assume that the price is ten shillings, then the makers receive nine shillings and the retailers one shilling. Now if, owing to over-supply, the wholesale price falls to eight shillings, it is obvious that makers will only receive eight shillings and the retailers will receive two shillings; under these circumstances the makers only get 8-10ths of the ultimate product instead of 9-10ths as formerly. Since makers derive their money income exclusively from making, it is obvious that this fall in wholesale prices reduces the value to them of the articles they make by 1-9th; that is to say, if they turn out x goods, receiving in exchange y commodities, they will now receive only $\frac{8y}{9}$ commodities in exchange for the old total of goods (x).

The same argument holds good if we assume that though retail prices fall, they do not fall to the same extent as wholesale; thus, if we assume a fall of 33⅓ per cent. in wholesale prices (less than the fall that has actually taken place between 1873 and to-day), whilst retail prices have only fallen ten per cent., then the ten-shilling article will be retailed at nine shillings; but as the wholesale price of this article has fallen from nine shillings to six shillings (33⅓ per cent.), the maker will only receive 6-9ths of the ultimate product instead of 9-10ths as formerly. The fall in wholesale prices relatively to retail is evidently the difference in the rates of fall (the difference between 33⅓ per cent. and ten per cent. = 23⅓ per cent.). We may, therefore, for the purposes of this argument, assume that retail prices are unchanged, and that wholesale prices have fallen 23⅓ per cent.

Now, if we assume that the Requisites of Production are distributed between making and retailing, in accordance with the reward derived from the two classes of trade, it follows that in the healthy condition of commerce 9-10ths of these requisites are applied to making and 1-10th to retailing; in the abnormal or unhealthy state, 6-9ths making and 3-9ths retailing. Now, if we assumed capital to be equally distributed amongst the individual members of the community, we can see (assuming each maker to make one article a day) that in a healthy state of commerce each individual would receive 9-10ths of an article daily, or, to get rid of fractions, every thirty individuals would receive twenty-seven articles. In the unhealthy state each individual would receive 6-9ths of an article, or every thirty individuals would receive twenty articles daily. Applying these figures to England, and assuming that there is no variation in prices and that the annual income is £. 1,000,000,000, in a healthy condition of commerce the annual income would be £. 1,350,000,000. Since, for reasons subsequently to be examined, the major part of this difference would be added to labourers' wages, and since such wages are estimated to amount to only £. 300,000,000 annually, the great importance of variations in wholesale prices relatively to retail to the working classes is sufficiently obvious. We do not argue that the fall in wholesale prices that has admittedly occurred does in actual fact mean a fall in wholesale prices relatively to retail of 23⅓ per cent.; it may mean more or it may mean less, but we do insist on the enormous importance of such variations, and on the fact, that would not, we apprehend, be denied, that wholesale prices are lower relatively to retail to-day than they were in 1873, and that to this extent the working classes must be injured by the fall.

It will be noticed that the increased total produced in a healthy commercial state over that produced in an unhealthy one does not involve the existence of more labourers or more capital, but merely that the old total is more effectively employed.

In concluding this chapter we wish to guard against any misconception of that portion of our argument which has assigned the Franco-German War as a cause of commercial prosperity. War is not necessarily 'good for trade'; in a healthy commercial condition of society, where the productive energies are vigorously engaged in keeping pace with a constantly growing consumption, war can be nothing else than an unmitigated evil. Only where and when there is a tendency towards an undue multiplication of forms of capital through an excessive desire to save, does War perform a real service to commerce by giving a temporary use to the otherwise useless and excessive forms of capital. By dwelling on this contingent advantage we claim to have offered a more satisfactory explanation than has hitherto been given of the extraordinary rapidity with which national commerce appears to recover from the terrible losses inflicted by long and disastrous wars. We are far from advocating war as a convenient remedy for commercial depression, but just as an artificial mode of depletion may on occasion be useful in ridding the physical body of excessive and unhealthy growths, so the commercial body, swollen with an undue accumulation of capital, may be relieved by being thus 'let blood.' Just as men who live a moderate and healthy life, neither overfeeding nor over-exerting themselves, and thus maintaining a true proportion between the production and consumption of animal flesh and force, are only injured by such violent and artificial modes of depletion, so a nation which, while exerting its productive powers to the full, is willing to raise its consumption continually, so as to keep pace with the increased rate of production, is in a healthy commercial condition, and needs no artificial outlet for its productive energy. If, however, a nation or a community will not consent to consume all it can produce (allowing for due cautious reservations) in the ordinary ways of expenditure, the congestion brought about must vent itself in some extraordinary way, or the community suffers incessantly from the functional diseases which such congestion brings.

It is, of course, obvious that if the community, instead of expending its surplus accumulations in the endeavour to cut its members' throats, consented to increase its consumption of luxuries, or applied the surplus funds to the improvement of the condition of the working classes or the sanitation of its great towns, all the contingent economic advantages of a war would be reaped, and the direct advantage of increased consumption of luxuries, of an improved condition of labourers, or of sanitary towns would be obtained.

CHAPTER VI.

THE LAW OF THE LIMITING REQUISITE.

IN the emphasis laid by most economists upon the fundamental antagonism between the interests of Labour, Capital, and Natural Agents, one most important factor in the problem has been slighted or altogether overlooked. In so far as the prime object of an income is to provide utilities and conveniences to its recipient, it is clear that the income of the community must vary with the amount of these utilities or conveniences that are produced; that is to say, must vary with the total of Commodities. If a full and economical use of the Requisites of Production enlarges the aggregate of production, as was the case in the period of the Franco-German War, the income of the Community rises; if a more wasteful use of these Requisites of Production diminishes the aggregate of production, as in the years of Depression subsequent to 1873, the income of the Community falls. It would seem naturally to follow that, inasmuch as Labour, Capital, and Natural Agents co-operate in the production of Commodities, they would share the gain or loss ensuant on the rise or fall of that fund out of which is paid the income each of them receives; that is to say, the total of Commodities produced forms a single wages-profits-rent fund, and it would be reasonable to think that all those who were paid for work done in common out of this common fund would gain by every rise and lose by every fall in the amount of this fund. This identity of interests has been affirmed by economic experience as often as it has been denied by economic theory. Those who have maintained a clash of interests traceable to a fundamental law have been continually brought face to face with commercial facts which give them the lie. Holding that as profits rise wages fall, and, *vice versâ*, that as rent rises profits fall, and so forth, they have been everywhere confronted with bursts of prosperity and adversity in which the gain or suffering has been shared by all three, or with instances of slow and steady advances or declines of commerce which seemed to affect Labour, Capital, and Land in the same way and in something like the same proportion. But here, as elsewhere, the complexity in the working of commercial forces makes it almost impossible to use experience so as to form legitimate inductions. In dealing with any larger economic subject we have not that thorough knowledge of conditions, that power of isolating phenomena, or, in general, that large and accurate record of series of facts, which are indispensable to the just application of the inductive method. It is for this reason that the most valuable and, rightly speaking, the most practical work in economics has been conducted on what logicians term the 'deductive method,' experience being used to verify or confute the conclusions derived from the application of large and universally recognised premisses.

Applying this method to our present subject of inquiry, we have to ask ourselves whether the fact that Wages, Profits, Rent, the sources of all individual income, are paid by partition of the total amount of commodities produced, is a sufficient guarantee that the interests of the three are identical. If we find that wages, profit, rent, do all rise with the amount of Commodities, we have further to ask if all gain in the same proportion. One question really underlies these two inquiries, What determines the proportion of the total Income which falls to Labour, Capital, Land, respectively? Now, it has been shown that Wages, Profits, Rent, are in every case payment for the Use of a Requisite of Production. Let us take a single commodity, a pair of boots. We have seen that when a pair of boots is sold to a consumer the price of it is divided and given as payment to all those who assist in replacing it. In so far as the labourers or capitalists who have assisted to produce a pair of boots have been paid for their services before the particular pair of boots was sold by the retailer, they will none the less receive their share of the money paid for this particular pair of boots as profit or wages for value put into another pair of boots in the ordinary course of trade, and the actual amount they will receive for value imparted to the second pair of boots is determined by the amount of purchase-money received by the retailer for the first pair For we have seen that it is the Demand of the consumer and the money by which he enforces his demand that determines and provides all the money incomes of those who in any way assist in producing the commodity he buys. Although, therefore, as a fact in commercial history, the money paid to the shoe-seller may be paid over to labourers at different points as wages for labour put into other pairs of shoes, it is none the less right to insist that these labourers receive a portion of the value of the pair of boots which has been sold by the retailer.

This division and payment is obscured by the complex nature of commerce, but it is an economic fact. Owners of Labour, Capital, and Natural Agents have all contributed to the production of this pair of boots by providing the Use of a Requisite of Production. In what proportion is the value of the pair of boots divided amongst them? It will be clear that this proportion depends on two conditions:—First, the amount of the Use of the Requisite of Production which each has contributed; second, the market price of the use of such Requisite of Production.

First. If a general improvement in bootmaking machinery rendered every £. 100 worth of machinery able to turn out twice as many boots as before, it is clear that the amount of use of machinery stored in each pair of boots would be half as much as formerly. Hence, assuming a full competition, the share of the value of the pair of shoes which fell to the Shoe manufacturer would be half what it was before. So, if by some miracle the efficiency of each workman were doubled so that he could by the same effort (*i.e.*, by the same amount of use of his

Requisite of Production) assist in producing twice the number of boots, the proportion of each pair which fell to him as wages would be half what it was before. Conversely, if twice as much of the use of any Requisite of Production were put in a commodity, the amount returned in payment for this use would be doubled. To this fact is due that large difference between retail and wholesale prices during periods of depressed trade. When two persons give their full energies to selling the same amount of goods which one person sufficed to sell before, the amount of retail labour represented in each article sold is twice what it was before. Thus, each pair of shoes sold contains twice as much use of retail labour as before, and consequently a larger proportion of the price paid by the purchaser goes to retail trade. So, previously, when the sudden increased Demand of the war stimulated making and reduced retailing to a minimum, the amount of retail labour in each commodity was very slight, and the difference between wholesale and retail price was very slight. But although, other things being equal, the amount of Use of each particular Requisite of Production stored in a commodity determines the proportion which is paid to the owner of that Requisite, it must be remembered that it does not follow that a high rate of payment to the owner of any Requisite means a high income for him. The amount of his income depends on the proportion he gets of each commodity he helps to produce, multiplied by the number of those commodities. When the total number of Commodities is much diminished, it is possible for the owner of any Requisite of Production to get an increased proportion of the value of each commodity, and at the same time to receive a less aggregate income, because he is not able to use his Requisite of Production in assisting the production of as many Commodities as he did before.

Second. But there is another consideration allied closely with the preceding, another condition which operates, along with the one described, to determine the rate of incomes received as Wages, Profits, Rent. In paying for the Use of a Requisite of Production, as in every other payment, we do not always pay the same price for the same amount. So the amount of each Requisite of Production stored in a Commodity is not the only consideration which regulates the apportionment of the Commodity among those who have helped to produce it. The market price of the Use of a Requisite of Production varies in accordance with the same law which, acting primarily on the price of Commodities, regulates the price of all things which are the subject of purchases—the Law of Supply and Demand. This Law applies in this wise: If the Quantity of the Use of Labour or Capital or Natural Agents demanded would exceed the Supply at the current price, the price, Wages, Profits, or Rent, rises; if the Supply at the current price would exceed the Quantity demanded, the price falls. Since every increase in Consumption or Quantity of Commodities demanded is an increased quantity of the use of each and all of the Requisites of Production demanded, it follows that every increase in Consumption should raise the prices of the Use of all three Requisites of Production. And this we find attested beyond all doubt by the facts of commerce. The increased demand of 1870–73 brought to all owners of Requisites of Production higher prices as payment for their use, wages were high, profits were high, rent was high. And this continued as long as the abnormal demand lasted. When the depression set in there followed a corresponding decline of wages, profits, rent. This decline was, as we have seen, due to an insufficiency of consumption, or, in other words, to a refusal of consumers to exert the full purchasing power that they possessed. The difference in the rate of incomes of the Community at the height of prosperity and the lowest depths of the depression was exactly represented by the difference in the amount of Commodities produced and consumed relatively to the quantity that could have been produced and consumed.

But although in the period of prosperity each owner of a Requisite of Production got larger payment because the use of his Requisite of Production was embodied in a larger quantity of Commodities, of each of which he received his due share, it by no means follows that the respective owners of the three Requisites of Production gained equally by the increased demand. When an increased Demand for Commodities calls for a proportionate increase of Requisites of Production by raising the price for their use, it does not follow that this price rises at an equal rate in all three cases. What makes the difference is the comparative ease or difficulty of increasing the Supply of each Requisite of Production respectively. If the increased quantity of Labour or Capital can be brought into use almost as easily as the quantity already in use, the price of the use of it will rise but slightly ; if it is more difficult to increase the quantity of Capital than of Labour the price of the use of Capital will rise more quickly. The comparative difficulty of increasing the quantity of equally effective Natural Agents has been long recognised as the cause of the rise of rent. When the increased demand acts as a strain upon the resources of existing Requisites of Production, the comparative tenseness of this strain is the measure of the rise in price of the use of each Requisite of Production. In other words, if there is one of the three Requisites of Production which cannot be reproduced or increased in quantity as rapidly as the other two, any increase of Consumption soon makes itself felt as a strain upon this Requisite of Production exclusively, and since the tenseness of the strain is the measure of the rise of price, the whole rise of price will be monopolised by that Requisite of Production which comes alone to bear this strain. If labour and capital are capable of easy and indefinite increase, while Natural Agents are less expansive, then the last may be said to form the barrier or limit to increase in production, and the whole increase in price of Commodities will be swallowed up in increased rent. This is the assumption on which the disciples of Henry George base their theory. If Natural Agents are practically without limit as to quantity and easy access, and the growth of population and the increased economy of labour due to the inventiveness of man makes it easy to get fresh labour, while Capital cannot be so easily increased, it is clear that Capital forms the limiting Requisite of Production, and that all increase in prices will eventually fall to Capital in increased Profits. This is the contention of Lasalle, Karl Marx, and those who hold the Iron Law of Wages.

Lastly. If Natural Agents and Capital admit of easy increase at a more rapid rate than Labour, the last will form the Limiting Requisite, and swallow up the rise of prices, that comes from increased demand, in higher wages.

This view of the relation of the three Requisites is what may be called the Law of the Limiting Requisite in Production.

It often happens that a sudden large increase in Consumption of some manufactured article makes itself felt almost equally as a strain upon the amount of Capital and of Labour already engaged in that manufacture, or readily available for such employment. Then the rise of price brought about by the increased Demand will cause an equal rise in the rate of wages and profits. As long as it continues equally difficult to increase the amount of Capital and of Labour in the requisite proportion which they economically bear, so long will the equal strain upon the two requisites be represented by an equal rise in wages and profits. When this rise is effectual in bringing an influx of new capital and new labour into the manufacture, it will generally be found that one flows in more freely than the other. Suppose that the labour is one which required special skill only to be acquired by an expensive training and years of practice, it is probable that a rise of profits would speedily attract as much capital as was required, while the rise of wages would act much more tardily in attracting labourers. In that case the strain which had at first been felt equally by Capital and Labour would subsequently fall exclusively on labour, and the latter would reap the whole advantage of any further rise up to the point when the height of wages would induce a flow of fresh labour, which was as free as the flow of capital into the new employment.

It is important to realise how this Law of the Limiting Requisite acts as a determinant of the rates of Wages, Profits, Rent. It is probable that when three Requisites of such a diverse character are essential to Production, that one or other of them will always, relatively to the others, be in short supply. Let us turn to Manufacture, and for the moment, setting aside considerations of rent, confine ourselves to the relations of Capital and Labour. First assume that production is limited by Capital, and that more labour is available than is required to work the various factories, railways, mines, &c., possessed by the community. Under these circumstances it is clear that the reward of the labourer, his wages, will not depend upon the gross amount of that portion of the stock of commodities which falls to those engaged in Manufacture, but solely upon the competition of those labourers who are out of employ. All those anxious to work cannot be employed because the Capital essential to their effective labour does not exist; these surplus labourers will therefore persistently continue to underbid those employed till wages have fallen to such a level that the unemployed surplus refuses to compete further. In all such periods, then, wages will be determined by the alternative means of subsistence which labourers have at their disposal. If these alternatives are more desirable, as in the colonies, where labourers can 'squat' or settle on unoccupied land, wash for gold, &c., the minimum of wages received will be relatively high. If these alternatives are less desirable, as in the East, where starvation is frequently the only alternative, the minimum of wages will be relatively low.[1] Since wages are, in all such periods, determined wholly without respect to the proportion of the total of Commodities which falls to Makers, and is represented by the wholesale price, it is evident that in the case of any increase in this proportion such increase will be retained by Capitalists in a rise of Profits.

If, on the other hand, production is limited by Labour, Capital existing in excess of the utmost required to assist the work of existing labourers, a section of Capitalists (those owning the unemployed or partially employed forms of Capital) will be unable to derive a reward, or the full reward, for the use of their Capital. These owners of surplus Capital will persistently compete for the assistance of labour (by raising wages) until so nearly the whole reward for production is paid to the labourers that Capitalists no longer care whether their Capital is used or not. In this case the labourers receive the whole of the wholesale price excepting the smallest fraction which a sufficient number of Capitalists will accept in preference to receiving nothing. In such a period it is

[1] It is generally acknowledged that the effect which the workhouse exerts on wages is very considerable; it prevents them from being driven below the point at which labour outside the House is less desirable than residence within it.

evident that the whole of any increase in the proportion of the total of Commodities which falls to Makers will be taken by the Labourers in higher wages. Lastly, suppose Natural Agents, or, for convenience, say Land, to be the Limiting Requisite. First take the simplest case of a community, entirely self-contained, occupying a country where all the good land is under cultivation and well worked. What would be the effect of a sudden increase in the quantity consumed? If we suppose there is plenty of labour and capital, either not fully used or which can be easily procured, of a quality equal or almost equal to that in use, the strain will come upon the land. That land which is already well cultivated will be worked still more thoroughly with a diminishing return to each portion of the fresh work applied to it, and inferior land will be put into cultivation. Until sufficient land has by these means been obtained to assist in supplying the increased Demand, the gradual rise of price occasioned by the strain upon existing Supply will be entirely swallowed up by the rise of rent, the payment for the use of the Limiting Requisite. Suppose that the quantity of inferior land, some of which is now brought into cultivation, is practically without limit, rent will not rise higher than this point, that is to say, when this inferior land begins to be called into use Land will cease to be the Limiting Requisite. Capital or Labour will now lay down the limit, and if the Demand still grows, any further rise of price will be swallowed up in higher profits or higher wages. Or, again, to come more nearly to existing facts, suppose that unappropriated Natural Agents, unlimited in quantity and of quality equal to those in use but situated in far-distant countries, can be had for the asking, in case of an increased Demand Land will continue to be the limiting requisite only up to the point where the rise of rent is equal to the sum necessary to induce the cultivation of this inconveniently situated land, and to pay for the transport of the products to the place where they are required. This is clearly illustrated in the development of English commerce. So long as our foreign trade was slight, any sudden increase in Demand for Commodities found the Limiting Requisite in Land; Labour and Capital were, comparatively speaking, plentiful, hence the rent of land continually rose. When the increased corn trade with America sprang up, agricultural rent in England was determined by the cost of producing corn in America of equal quality, *plus* the cost of transportation, *plus* the amount of the duty on imported corn. Now that the corn duty has been abolished, cost of transport diminished, new and large tracts of corn-growing country opened, the rent of English agricultural land has fallen, because it is no longer the requisite limiting our commercial growth. Land supplies the Raw Material out of which all manner of goods (including Agricultural produce) are formed, and the Machinery that helps to form them; so long as it is easier to obtain increased quantities of this Raw Material than it is to obtain increased quantities of either Labour or Capital, Land will not be a Limiting Requisite. The rent of land in or near towns has risen while agricultural rents have fallen, for the simple reason that convenience of position is more important in the one case than the other. The owner of land in a town has a monopoly, in so much as he can obtain, in addition to agricultural rent, that sum which competing tradesmen or other occupants are willing to pay in order that their factory or house may be in the centre of a large population, in preference to building it on land to be obtained outside a town at the agricultural rate.

If we look more in detail at commercial experience we shall find that the strain caused by an increase in consumption does not necessarily disclose at once the ultimate Limiting Requisite, but that at different stages of any such period each of the three Requisites may, in turn, form for a time the Limiting Requisite, may feel the tenseness of the strain, and may reap the reward of this pressure in an increased rate of payment. Reverting once more to the Franco-German War, let us note the order in which the strain was felt. As soon as Consumption (including the war waste) tended to exceed the utmost which Makers could replace, we saw that Makers received within a fraction of the whole value produced. But this did not show itself in an immediate and equivalent rise in the wages, profits, and rent of those who owned the Requisites of Production.

The first to reap the advantage was the Capitalist; profits rose enormously, while wages did not immediately rise to any considerable extent. Since the whole, or nearly the whole, of the enhanced wholesale price was retained by the Capitalist in a higher rate of profits, we may safely conclude that Capital at first formed the Limiting Requisite, and that there was in existence an unemployed surplus of labour which could be obtained for the same, or nearly the same, price as that received by labourers already in employment. It must be remembered that in tracing the commercial effects of the Franco-German War we are not looking so much at the belligerent countries themselves, as at the effects produced in England and other non-belligerent portions of the trading community. Capital figured as the one limiting requisite at the beginning of the increase in quantity demanded. So soon, however, as the labour demanded to construct fresh Plant, together with that demanded to work the fresh Plant, had absorbed the unemployed surplus of labourers, and all existing labour power obtained the fullest use, Capital no longer figured as the Limiting Requisite. Labour found itself in that position, and wages began to rise rapidly, moving towards that point when labourers would receive in wages the whole of the ultimate produce, less a minimum commission to retailers, and the minimum profit which Capitalists would consent to receive in preference to allowing their capital to stand idle. Before that point was reached, however, the decrease in quantity demanded, and consequent panic of 1873, brought about a collapse in prices the effects of which have already been noticed. If the war-rate of Consumption had continued or increased there is every reason to believe that labour would have continued to be the limiting requisite, and that wages would have reached and maintained a level far higher than that which they actually attained.

When the actual forms of Capital are considered, it is obvious that Capital does not possess that fluidity, or applicability to various purposes, assumed for it by economists. Thus a particular form of Capital, say a sewing machine, can only be applied to aid the production of clothing; or a particular form of Capital, raw cotton, can only be applied to the production of a particular class of commodities, and that class alone. There is in actual fact no fluidity whatever in forms of Capital; the general impression of fluidity which Capital gives being due, in part, to the rapidity with which new forms can be created, and in part to the facility with which individuals can exchange with each other the particular forms they own.

In dealing with the Franco-German War period we have seen how the increase in the quantity of particular classes of commodities demanded raised prices and profits, causing particular classes of forms of Capital to be the Requisites of Production limiting Industry. We have also seen how the desire to gain these high profits led saving individuals to demand the creation of these highly remunerated forms of Capital, and by so doing to continuously widen the circle of Requisites of Production which experienced the increased demand; and we have seen that the general rise in wages which marked 1872 and 1873 was due to the fact that the quantity of labour demanded:—(*a*) to work the Capital actually in existence (*b*) to create new Capital (open mines, reclaim land, construct railways, &c., &c.), exceeded the supply offered at the current price.

Though, therefore, certain special forms of capital held at the outset the position of limiting Requisite, this position was soon lost by Capital and gained by Labour, and had the quantity of Commodities demanded still reached the total economically desirable, the labourers would have been the Requisite of Production limiting Industry. They could then have dictated their own terms to the owners of Capital, terms limited only by the necessity that wages must not exceed the whole of the ultimate product, but must afford a margin of gain to the Capitalist sufficient to induce him to apply his Capital to aid production in preference to leaving it idle and receiving nothing.[1] So soon, however, as Production is limited, not by the total of any one or other of the Requisites of Production available for use, but by the aggregate that consumers will consent to buy and consume, there is no Requisite of Production which limits Industry. Surplus Labour, Capital, and Natural Agents exist, and the rates of wages, interest and profit, and rent are determined at the point at which a sufficiency, and no more, of each of these Requisites is offered for use, a point so low that the owners of the unused Labour, Capital, and Natural Agents no longer compete with those actually employed. The most efficient labourers, the most skilfully manipulated Capital, and the best Natural Agents are alone used; the less efficient Labour, Capital, and Natural Agents are an unused Surplus, and their owners must subsist otherwise than on these surplus and unused Requisites.

Since the experience of 1870, 1871, 1872, and 1873 has shown that Capital and Natural Agents would not, in the present state of society, be able to long maintain the position of limiting Requisites, it is obvious that a period of Depression in Trade does not materially injure their owners, though it is true

[1] Their position relatively to natural agents would have been that usually ascribed to them by economists, following the principle set forth in Ricardo s law of rent.

that if more Production were effected, more Capital and more Natural Agents would be used. But even in this latter case the rate of reward obtainable on any given total of Natural Agents or Capital would not presumably be largely affected for more than a very short period. Labour, however, is affected, and disastrously affected, by insufficiency in the quantity demanded. From being the Requisite of Production, limiting industry and receiving in consequence within a fraction of the whole of the ultimate product, it becomes a non-limiting Requisite, and receives the smallest fraction of the ultimate product which a section of its owners will accept in preference to receiving nothing and remaining idle.

Or, to state it otherwise, the limiting Requisite suffers from no competition; the quantity of its use that would be demanded is necessarily always in excess of the quantity offered, and, as a consequence, its owners have no need to compete with each other. When Labour is the limiting Requisite, the one limit to wages is the whole of the ultimate product, less certain minimum deductions. So soon, however, as Industry is restricted by reason of insufficient consumption, labourers are thrown out of work, and the rate of wages is fixed at the point at which even unemployed labourers cease to compete further; and, as we have seen, this point is determined wholly irrespective of the more or less of the ultimate product, and exclusively by the more or less desirable alternative methods of subsistence open to this unemployed surplus.[1]

[1] See page 173.

We are thus able to understand why all the modern improvements in machinery and the methods of production have failed to lighten the day's work of the labourer, or to have materially increased his control of subsistence, conveniences, and amusement.

The labourers' wages are determined in all periods of insufficient demand by the iron law, which says that, of the labourers able and willing to work, a section shall not work, and that those who work shall receive wages so low that those out of work would refuse to accept them. Wages, under these circumstances, are determined at the lowest conceivable point, and, so long as quantity demanded is insufficient, wages must remain there. The labourers, therefore, are the chief sufferers from the saving habits of the rich, and, in so far as evil proceeds from poverty, the highly-extolled virtues of thrift, parsimony, and saving are the cause.

In concluding, it may be well to sum up briefly the argument by which excessive Thrift has been thus related to Depression in Trade.

All money received by individuals in a commercial community is received as payment for the Use of Natural Agents, or Capital, or Labour engaged in forwarding the production of Commodities. A certain portion of this money must constantly be applied to replace the machinery and goods engaged in production at different points in the industrial machine, so as to maintain the present rate of production. So far as individuals fail to perform this task, and instead use the money in buying commodities, they are rightly described as living on their capital. All the rest of the money received, after the necessary deduction is made, is the money income. This money income may be employed either in acquiring possession of Commodities for personal consumption, or a portion only may be used in this way, while the rest is employed in obtaining possession of Plant, Machinery, and Raw Material, so as to produce a new set of Commodities in excess of that produced before. But though any individual may spend any proportion of his income in this last way, which is called Saving, the community, as a whole, can only spend a certain proportion of its income thus with advantage. For the utility of thus saving a portion of its income depends upon its willingness to spend another portion in buying for consumption the increased stock of Commodities which this 'Saved income' is engaged in producing. Thus the community can effect no useful end by saving and putting into the forms of capital a larger proportion of its income than is required to assist in producing what it is willing to purchase and consume with the other portion of its income. Yet we have seen that there is a force, namely, the individual desire of accumulation, which may impel a community, through the action of its individual members, to save a larger proportion of its income than is desirable. We have further seen that the increase of production thus brought about has no natural power to force such an increased consumption in the future as shall justify this apparent excess of saving by providing a fresh demand for the products which it assists to create. Thus the Over-Production engendered by excessive thrift can only be cured by a decline in the rate of production slowly brought about by a fall in profits. Such a decline in rate of production throws out of employment a portion of existing forms of capital, a portion of the natural agents formerly in use, and a number of labourers whose labour has no longer any use. Thus the incomes of the owners of all these requisites of production is diminished; that is, Rent, Wages, Profits fall, and we reach that industrial condition described as Depression of Trade.

In this Depression the owners of that Requisite which would otherwise have been the Requisite limiting Production suffer most severely. We have seen that the experience of the Franco-German War period conclusively shows that at the present period this Requisite would be Labour, and it is, therefore, the Labourers who have most to lose by the economic evils resulting from the excessive desire to amass fortunes.

Before quitting this subject we may just explain the apparent paradox, that while any individual can always save by reducing his consumption, the community, as a whole, cannot do so. The explanation is this: The reduction in consumption caused by the saving of the thrifty reduces all incomes, and this reduction of all incomes continuously proceeds until the least thrifty section of the community ceases to live on its incomes and begins to spend its Capital. So soon as this occurs an unlimited field of investment is opened to the thrifty. The forms of Capital previously owned by these 'extravagant' folk are purchased by the saving individuals, and form excellent investments for their savings. Since it is always possible for any individual to be more thrifty than his neighbours, it is always possible for an individual to save. It is quite true that such saving is not a saving as regards the whole community; but it does not matter to the accumulator of a fortune whether his fortune is an addition to the aggregate wealth of the community, or whether it is embodied in the forms previously belonging to other individuals, whom, by his saving operations, he has forced to live on their Capital. To make the operation of this law clearer, we will take the simplest possible case—that of a number of peasant proprietors paying a fixed money tax either to the State or to Landlords. Undue thrift in such a case would accumulate a surplus of all sorts of farm produce, and consequently prices would continuously fall; sooner or later the less thrifty of the peasants would be unable to provide the constantly increasing amounts of farm produce that would have to be sold to meet their fixed money payments; so soon as this occurred they would have to borrow from their more thrifty neighbours, and little by little the saving operations of these thrifty folk would eject them from their holdings, and reduce them to the position of labourers or tramps.

CHAPTER VII.

SCARCITY OF GOLD AS AN ECONOMIC FACTOR.

IT is asserted by economists of the currency school that price changes are induced by changes in the inherent value of gold, and that these price changes are the cause of depression in trade. We purpose in this chapter to ascertain whether there is any foundation for this contention in the facts, figures, and arguments on which and by which it is supported.

The arguments of this school are two in number: the first, that gold is scarce, and that this scarcity enhances its value; the second, that the cost of producing gold has risen, and that consequently the value of all the gold in existence has correspondingly risen. Taking the first of these contentions, we will endeavour to see whether scarcity of gold and low prices, and a plethora of gold and high prices, are, in actual fact, simultaneous phenomena.

At the outset of the inquiry, however, we must brush away any lingering traces of the old mercantile theory, which asserts that purchasing power, the power to purchase 'subsistence, conveniences, and amusement' inheres in gold. 'Purchasing power,' says Professor Cairnes, and no one, we believe, would dispute this statement, 'owes its existence to the production of a commodity, and, the conditions of industry being given, can only be increased by increasing the quantity of commodities offered for sale.' For instance, when a doctor is said to make £.1,500 a year, it means that he gives professional advice, &c., which he exchanges with his patients for that sum. When he goes into a shop and buys any article, he really pays for it by the professional services he has previously rendered some other individual. He, every year, produces professional services valued at £.1,500, and he, every year, receives commodities valued at £.1,500 a year; or, if he prefers it, he, instead of taking his whole income in commodities, may take part in capital, and thus 'save for future advantage.' The value of his services temporarily stored up in coins, or in a banker's credit, he transfers to the sellers of such articles as he desires; in other words, he spends or exerts the purchasing power he has created. Similarly, the incomes of all other individuals (excluding gold miners) can invariably be shown to be derived from production, the money being merely the cart or vehicle which conveys this purchasing power from its producers to the particular fraction of supply on which they desire to exert it as a demand.

This carting or conveyance of purchasing power from one individual to another is the only use of currency. It is for this purpose, and this alone, that banks, with all their apparatus of bills and cheques, and drafts and acceptances, &c., &c., exist. It is for this purpose, and this alone, that governments mint the gold and silver into coins. It is for this purpose, and this alone, that the national banks store up the great masses of bullion which they call reserves.

The one object of production being to get useful and convenient things into the hands of consumers, money assists the process in the following way. When an individual has produced a useful or convenient thing which he does not want to consume himself, money enables the community to enjoy the consumption of it at once, without waiting for the producer to find some one else who wants the article, and who at the same time has in his possession something else which the first-mentioned individual desires to have. To prevent the delay and trouble of a system of direct barter, it is arranged that when a person has produced anything he shall give it up to the use of any other member of the community who shall give him a guarantee, which shall enable him, at any future time, to obtain from some other person that which he would be willing to take in exchange for what he has sold. Money, then, assists in conveying ownership by means of a system of guarantees. Products are still exchanged for products, but by means of money each exchanging party is able to get the equivalent of the product he offers in any form and at any time, instead of taking it in one form and at the time when some one else desires it, who has something he wants. Products possess purchasing power, but when this power exists in a special form it is not fully and easily operative. The sale of a product for money is, on the part of the seller, the exchange of a special form of purchasing power for a general form of purchasing power, conveyed in the form of that token called money. The service rendered the community by money is, therefore, though of great importance, of a strictly limited character. It facilitates exchanges, enabling the clumsy and tedious system of direct barter to be replaced by the easy and convenient system of indirect barter, *i.e.*, selling for money and purchasing with money. It must, however, never be forgotten that this money system is only an elaborated barter system. Products still exchange for products, though the exchange is not direct, but consists of products for money and money for products. Money, while it obscures, in no wise changes the facts of barter, and its use is limited to the aid it gives to the exchange of commodities.

It is next necessary to ascertain whether gold is, as alleged by the Bimetallists, scarce. For this purpose we will first consider what is the meaning of the term 'demand for money.' We have seen (Chapter III.) that the only demand which the community can exert is a demand for consumable articles by consumers, all other so called demands being resolvable, when regarded from the community's point of view, into mere changes in individual ownership. Currency, therefore, cannot be demanded; the community possesses exactly the same number of sovereigns whether any given sovereign is in the pocket of A. or B., or C., or in the cellars of the Bank of England. What, then, is meant by 'demand for money'? The answer is plain; it is a demand for the use of money. Just as we showed that what is commonly but erroneously called demand for capital is really a demand for the use of capital, so we now see that the so-called demand for money is a demand for the use of money. Banks sell the use of money and they purchase the use of money; the price of this use they term the rate of discount (or more usually Bank rate). Now, applying our law of price, we can see that if the quantity of this use demanded increases relatively to the supply, Bank rate rises; if the quantity of this use demanded decreases relatively to the supply, Bank rate falls. The correspondence of Bank rate, or the price of the use of money, with variations in the quantity of the use of gold currency demanded relatively to the supply available, is well illustrated by the following table, taken from Mr. Giffen's 'Essays in Finance:'—

Year.	Reserve in Millions Sterling.		Rate of Discount.
	Above Average.	Below Average.	
			£. s. d.
1872 - - -	—	12·1	4 2 0
1873 - - -	—	12·0	4 15 10
1874 - - -	—	11·0	3 14 1
1875 - - -	—	11·5	3 4 8
1876 - - -	15·9	—	2 12 1
1877 - - -	—	12·4	2 18 0
1878 - - -	—	10·8	3 15 8
1879 - - -	18·4	—	2 7 6
1880 - - -	16·0	—	2 15 0
1881 - - -	13·7	—	3 10 0
1882 - - -	—	11·8	4 2 6
1883 - - -	—	12·4	3 11 3
1884 - - -	—	13·3	2 19 0

A comparison with earlier figures adduced by Mr. Giffen serves most strongly to emphasise the point which the figures above sufficiently indicate, that during the years of Scarcity of Gold, when the Bank Reserve has been abnormally low, the rate of discount has been high; and that within this period the rate of discount has generally varied inversely with the amount of the Reserve. It may be observed that exact correspondence between rate of discount and amount of Reserve is not to be expected, for the former is strictly determined by the risk attending loans, and this risk is determined not exclusively by the condition of the Bank Reserve, but is also affected by considerations which relate to the general condition of trade and the average credit of borrowers. But the main fact that scarcity of Gold currency raises the rate of discount is clearly established.

Now, the only ground on which it appears possible to argue that gold is scarce, is on the assumption that the quantity of gold available for use as currency is less than the quantity which it is desirable should be so available. Gold currency is obviously of no use unless used, and a 'scarcity' of gold must mean that there is a lack or insufficiency of gold for currency purposes. The 'scarcity' of gold, therefore, which the Bimetallists and others argue is the cause of the present low range of prices and Depression in Trade, can only mean that the quantity of gold currency available for use is less than the quantity of gold currency which it is desirable should be available for use. If this 'scarcity' is the cause of low prices, the converse must be equally true, and high prices must be caused by a relative plethora of gold currency. We have already seen that the Bank rate of discount is the price of the use of gold currency, and, reverting to our law of price, we can assert that if the quantity of this use demanded increases relatively to the supply available (if, in short, gold is scarce), Bank rate must rise; if, on the other hand, the quantity of this use demanded decreases relatively to the supply, Bank rate must fall. 'Scarcity,' therefore, will be accurately gauged by

Bank rate; if gold currency is relatively scarce, Bank rate will be high; if it be relatively plentiful, Bank rate will be low. To ascertain whether low prices and scarce gold, and high prices and plentiful gold, are, as the Bimetallists and others urge, interdependent phenomena, we will again borrow from Mr. Giffen, the most influential exponent of this doctrine, and show by his own figures that, on the contrary, scarce gold and high prices, and plentiful gold and low prices, are in actual fact invariably co-existent :—

Year.	Index No.	Bank Reserve in Millions Sterling.	Rate of Discount. £. s. d.
1865 - - -	3575———	8·0———	4 15 4
1866 - - -	3564———	6·7———	6 19 0
1867 - - -	3024	12·9	2 10 9
1868 - - -	2682	11·9	2 1 11
1869 - - -	2662	10·3	3 4 2
1870 - - -	2689	12·4	3 2 0
1871 - - -	2590	14·1	2 17 8
1872 - - -	2835———	12·1 ———	4 2 0
1873 - - -	2947———	12·0 ———	4 15 10
1874 - - -	2891	11·0	3 14 1
1875 - - -	2778	11·5	3 4 5
1876 - - -	2711	15·9	2 12 1
1877 - - -	2715	12·4	2 18 0
1878 - - -	2554	10·8	3 15 8
1879 - - -	2202	18·4	2 7 6
1880 - - -	2538	16·0	2 15 0
1881 - - -	2376	13·7	3 10 0
1882 - - -	2435———	11·8———	4 2 6
1883 - - -	2342	12·4	3 11 3
1884 - - -	2221	13·3	2 19 0

The column of Index Numbers represents the condition of general prices, and is obtained by taking averages of the prices of representative products during the year. The other columns require no explanation. The black line is drawn to denote years in which the rate of discount is above £.4. It will here be seen that the high rate of discount has in every case co-existed with a higher price level than in the neighbouring years of low discount. The dotted lines denote years in which the bank reserve averaged above fourteen millions ; in three cases out of four prices were lowest when bank reserve was highest. The five years of highest bank-rate (average of five years, £.4 18*s.* 11*d.*) give a price level of 3,071, while the six years of lowest bank-rate (average of six years, £.2 10*s.* 9*d.*) give a price level of 2,624. The bank reserve during these same years averages 14·8 for the price level of 2,624 and 10·2 for the price level of 3,071.

In the face of facts like these, can it be argued that insufficiency of gold causes low prices ? or, that plethora of gold causes high prices ? or, that high rate of discount lowers prices, while low rate raises them ? Mr. Giffen appears to be partly aware that his figures do not adequately support his theory, and endeavours to argue that the effect of a fall in discount will not be felt immediately on prices ; a rise of discount to-day to ten per cent. would not, he contends, cause me and other traders to take lower prices to-day, but to take lower prices next year, or in two or three years' time, when the rate of discount has, perhaps, fallen to two per cent. But this extraordinary contention is, we take it, only the result of Mr. Giffen finding that his figures do not tally with his theory. If he had found low prices actually coincident with high rates of discount and the converse, we should have heard nothing of any reason why the effects should be postponed. Any impartial examiner of the figures we have quoted will come to the conclusion that scarcity of gold and high rates of discount are not the cause of low prices.[1]

We have seen that the only demand which can be exerted for gold currency is a demand for its use, and that the price of this use falls when other prices fall, and rises when other prices rise. The reason is obvious; gold is a mere tool, or machine, to aid and facilitate the work of production, and the same cause which depresses the prices paid for the uses of the other requisites of production, depresses the price paid for the use of currency. We are not here dealing with the very involved problem of how the normal rate of interest is determined, but merely with those temporary fluctuations on which the Bimetallists rely for an explanation both of depression in trade and low prices.

We have next to consider the second theory advanced by the Bimetallists, that the cost of producing gold has increased, and that consequently the value of all the gold in existence has risen. They

[1] Since this was written, Mr. Giffen has receded from the position taken by him in his "Essays on Finance;" he now asserts the conclusion to which our argument leads, *i.e.*: "There is a relation between the quantity of money and prices, but it is rather one in which prices assist in determining the quantity of the precious metals to be used as money, and not one in which prices are themselves determined by that quantity." "A Problem in Money." Mr. Giffen, "Nineteenth Century," November 1889.

argue in this wise: the cost of producing the most expensively-grown wheat required to supply the "last margin of consumption" determines the price of wheat. They then apply this argument to currency gold, without, however, perceiving that its validity rests exclusively on the assumption that the most expensively produced gold is required "to supply the last margin of consumption." Now, we have seen that currency gold is not consumed; all that is consumed is its use, and so far is it from the fact that this most expensively produced gold is required for use, *i.e.*, is required "to supply the last margin of consumption," that, on the contrary, gold currency has been persistently more abundant relatively to the quantity required for use, during the years marked by low prices and Depression in Trade than during the years marked by high prices," and a "prosperity advancing by leaps and bounds." The most expensively produced gold has not, therefore, been produced, as the Bimetallists fondly imagine, to supply the "last margin of consumption," but has been produced to lie idle in the vaults of the great national banks, and the cost of producing it has, therefore, had nothing to do with the value of gold.

While, however, the cost of producing gold does not determine prices, prices do determine the cost of producing gold. For instance, if the product of the use of certain capital and labour sells for one ounce weight of gold, and if similar totals of the use of capital and labour applied to crushing quartz yielding one ounce of gold to the ton of stone would produce one ounce of gold in the same time and with the same effort, then it will be indifferent to the capitalist and labourers whether they crush quartz or produce commodities. In either case they obtain equal totals of gold, and consequently of general purchasing power. If, however, general prices fall to one-half, the labour and capital applied to the production of commodities will only produce a product selling for half an ounce of gold, and it will in consequence 'pay' these requisites of production to crush any quartz that yields more than half an ounce of gold to the ton. By producing commodities they only get half an ounce of gold. So long, therefore, as quartz yielding more than this half ounce can be found, capital and labour will be devoted to work it. But the application of labour, &c., to the crushing of inferior quartz is, of course, equivalent to a rise in the cost of production of gold, a fall in general prices is, therefore, immediately operative in raising the cost of producing gold, and were prices to fall to one-tenth of their present level, quartz which required ten times as much expenditure of the use of capital and labour would be brought into requisition. So it would still be found that the most expensively produced gold only just paid its cost of production. There is absolutely no limit to the cost at which gold could be produced, and what this cost shall be is determined and determined exclusively by the general retail price level.

The law of price asserted on page 81 is, we can thus see, irrefutable by either of the arguments of the currency school. So long as the sellers of commodities can sell all they have to offer at the current price, prices cannot fall, and this holds good equally, whether gold is scarce or plentiful. Sellers do not trouble to ask any question as to the state of the Bank reserve, or the cost at which gold is being produced. All they care to know is, whether they can sell everything they have to offer at the current price. If they believe they can, neither scarcity of gold, nor cost of gold, nor anything to do with gold, will induce them to take a lower price. If, on the other hand, they believe that they will not be able to sell all they have to offer at the current price, then prices will fall, no matter how plentiful gold may be, or to what depth its cost of production may have fallen.

It does not matter how much money there may be in existence or in the banks, or even in the pockets of private individuals, prices are affected only by the application of purchasing power as a Demand.

The mere fact of an increase or decrease in the amount of existing money in a community can have no effect on prices. If the amount of money in everyone's purse were miraculously doubled, why should that fact oblige anyone to pay more for a loaf of bread or a hat? The baker sold me a loaf for threepence before; how will he be able now to induce me to pay sixpence, or even fourpence? He will make his usual profit on the sale if I pay him threepence as before, and the competition of other bakers will prevent him making more than the usual profit. So with the hatter. If everyone resolves to use no more money than before this miraculous increase and behaves as if he had not got it, no rise in price will occur. It is only when the possession of more money induces people to try to buy more loaves or more hats, to apply more purchasing power to buy goods at current prices, that they will find these prices rise. It is only when these shopkeepers perceive that they could sell at current prices more goods than they have got that they raise their prices, and sell all they have at a little higher price. So a fall of price will only be brought about when the shopkeeper perceives that a smaller number of people than usual are offering to buy loaves or hats at the usual prices. When the case is thus concretely put it will be obvious that no change of price can come in any other way than by an alteration in the ratio which Supply bears to the Quantity demanded.

Though the more or less of the gold currency in existence has nothing to do with the determination of general price levels, the entry of gold into circulation does to some extent affect them. It is, therefore, desirable, before quitting this subject, to glance at the method in which such effects are caused, and to note the limitations to which they are necessarily subject.

The way in which gold comes into circulation is this: Governments give to gold miners or their representatives an amount of general purchasing power, in the shape of money or notes, in return for the gold they bring. This general purchasing power, according as it is used or is not used by the miners, has its effect in increasing or diminishing the aggregate quantity of commodities demanded upon which prices depend.

If in any given year the same body of gold producers doubles the amount of gold they furnish the Government, and consequently receive twice as much power to purchase as before, the full exercise of this increased power to demand will raise prices to the extent necessary to restore the proper ratio between the aggregate supply and the aggregate demanded. In the same way any decrease in the amount of gold added to the currency in any year will so far affect prices in that it diminishes the amount of quantity demanded to an extent corresponding with the amount of the decrease. Thus, if in any year the amount of gold added to that available for currency purposes exceeds the average amount by two millions, the only effect on price is through an increase in quantity demanded to the extent of two millions, assuming supply to be stable. If, as is actually alleged, during the last fifteen years the yearly addition of gold to our currency is £. 2,000,000 less than it ought to be in order to maintain the same proportion between gold currency and volume of trade, the general effect on prices is limited to the effect produced by a decline of £. 2,000,000 in quantity demanded in relation to a fixed supply. This diminution of £. 2,000,000 in quantity demanded represents a fall in the aggregate amount of purchasing power handed over to gold miners in return for gold, and it presumes that the same amount of capital and labour has been engaged in the production of the smaller amount of gold as was formerly engaged in producing a larger amount.

But, suppose that those engaged in the production of gold, finding that they can no longer produce the same amount of gold as before with the same expenditure of capital and labour, that the amount they are able to supply to England has sunk from $3\frac{1}{4}$ millions to $1\frac{3}{4}$ millions, act in accordance with the general action of commerce, what will be the result? An amount of which capital and labour, formerly was able to produce £. 2,000,000 of gold, is gradually removed from gold production,[1] and is applied to some other productive work, whereby we have a right to assume £. 2,000,000 worth of new supply is created. These quondam gold miners now possess the same amount of purchasing power as they did when they were engaged in producing gold, say, £. 2,000,000, and the total amount of purchasing power possessed by the community is the same as before. On the other hand, the aggregate of supply (excluding gold) has been increased by the £. 2,000,000 fresh supply contributed by our quondam gold miners. Hence the total disturbance in the relations of supply and quantity demanded is still limited to £. 2,000,000.

Assuming that when gold production falls from 3¾ millions to 1¾ millions, the same amount of the requisites of production are still employed in producing this smaller aggregate result, while the aggregate supply of the community (excluding gold) remains as before, the total purchasing power and, assuming it to be all used, the total quantity demanded, is decreased by two millions. On the other hand, suppose the requisites of production formerly engaged in gold production are applied with equal efficacy to some other production, the total producing power and the total quantity demanded remain as before, but supply is increased by two millions. Thus the direct effect of this fall off in gold production upon price

[1] If it be objected by 'practical' readers that capital invested in mines cannot be removed, we need only remind them that as the forms of capital need constant renewal, the abstention from such renewal comes to the same thing as the actual withdrawal of existing capital.

is in no case greater than is to be accounted for by an addition of £. 2,000,000 to the total supply, or a subtraction of the same amount from the total of quantity demanded.

Now, let us ask to what extent this can affect prices? The total income of the United Kingdom has been estimated by Mr. Leone Levi to be about £. 1,270,000,000, and Mr. Giffen accepts that figure as a minimum.[1] This sum then, represents the total purchasing power, the demand power of the community; and, assuming a stable condition of supply, any increase or decrease of this sum will affect general prices proportionately. Now, the whole alleged effect of the scarcity of gold is to diminish this grand total by £. 2,000,000. The fall of prices thus brought about could only be to the extent of $\frac{2}{1270}$, or less than $\frac{1}{6}$th per cent., for by that amount alone is the aggregate quantity demanded reduced. Yet the scarcity in gold has been adduced as an explanation of a general fall in prices amounting to not less than thirty per cent.[2] between the years 1872 and 1885.

[1] Giffen "Essays in Finance," p. 460 (note).
[2] Giffen "Essays in Finance," p. 19.

CHAPTER VIII.

PRACTICAL CONSIDERATIONS.

ANYONE who has carefully perused the foregoing chapters will perceive that the theory therein set forth will, if it be correct, admit and indeed demand certain practical applications which are opposed to the whole tenour of economic legislation. With regard to the statement of these practical considerations we are in the following dilemma. If we refrain from all such statement we shall lay ourselves open to the imputation of being blind to certain practical issues which will seem on first sight to furnish a *reductio ad absurdum* reply to our argument. On the other hand, if we attempt to lay much stress upon what we hold to be inevitable practical deductions from our theory, we shall be driven into long and intricate lines of defence which, from the very importance of the issues with which they deal, will divert the attention of the reader from the theoretic basis of the earlier chapters. Moreover, while we feel confident that the theoretic basis of this work will stand the test of close criticism, we are by no means sure that, in attempting to apply these principles fairly to the intricate system of commercial facts, we shall successfully avoid all those fallacies which all economists find in the work of their fellows, and which, when disclosed, are often unjustly, though not unnaturally, held to impair the correctness of the main principles from which they are incorrectly deduced.

It has, therefore, seemed wisest to us to make a brief and general statement of those practical tendencies and conclusions which seem justified by our theory, and to leave the fuller exposition and defence of them for a future occasion. If these practical considerations seem to involve much that is startling and somewhat that is retrograde, we would urge that we have endeavoured, in accordance with the advice of Plato, 'to follow whithersoever the argument shall lead us.'

1. It will be evident that the question of method of taxation, in so far as it bears upon the rate of consumption and of saving, will be directly affected by the foregoing theory. In all periods of under-consumption (*i.e.*, of low prices and depressed trade) taxation should clearly be directed so as to be the smallest check upon consumption. Since under-consumption has been traced to an excessive desire to save, a rational method of taxation will aim at restricting the motive to save, while offering every encouragement to the desire to spend.

The tendency of taxation in England is based upon the opposite principle ; it seeks to restrict consumption by artificially raising the price of certain commodities classed under the name of luxuries. Beer, wine, spirits, tobacco, tea, plate, carriages, horses, railway-tickets, &c., are all more or less heavily taxed, in most cases with the avowed intention of checking consumption. So, again, the income-tax is levied so as to operate in the same way. If an individual will consent to save a portion of his income and apply it to insuring his life, this portion of his income is exempted from income-tax with the avowed object of encouraging thrift. The indirect and unintentional effect of the mode of levying the income-tax makes in the same direction. The expenditure of an individual attracts the attention of the assessors, and ensures the full assessment; on the other hand, an individual who lives penuriously frequently evades the tax merely because he is a saving man. Thus we see that our methods of direct and indirect taxation operate to check expenditure and encourage saving. When the existence of under-consumption proves the operation of an excessive desire to save, it is evident that taxation should rightly be directed to check saving, and not expenditure, and should fall on that portion of the individual's income which he refuses to spend. Other legislative enactments which operate in the same manner are the laws of entail and settlement. The only possible advantages which can be claimed for these laws are that individuals are thereby prevented from spending more than their incomes; they are deterrents of extravagance and waste.

Since the supposition of a state of under-consumption implies that any increase in the quantity demanded, whatever be the nature of the commodities demanded, will have a beneficial effect upon commerce by providing a use for an increased quantity of the Requisites of Production, it will follow that the full stress of all taxation should fall on accumulated property, so as to check the creation of fresh stocks of unneeded and injurious Capital. To put it in a single phrase, all forms of Savings should be taxed.

Any reader who, without troubling himself with the preceding argument should turn to the last chapter to see 'what the book is about,' should cast his eye upon this sentence, will doubtless pronounce the notion preposterous, and will read no more. But all who have followed the course of the preceding chapters will be compelled to the acceptance of this first practical application. Where Under-consumption exists, Savings should be taxed. We have shown above that Under-consumption is no mere term to describe a momentary and occasional crisis, but rather describes a commercial malady which is chronic in the industrial life of modern European nations.

Without entering at length into the large question of Free Trade, it is right to indicate the bearing which the theory of Under-consumption has upon the practical issues involved. The advantage claimed for Free Trade rightly rests on the assumption that, in just proportion as there is freedom of competition among individuals, groups of individuals, or nations, in respect of production, the various Requisites of Production will be put to an effective use; that capital and labour, left without the artificial guidance and attraction of protective tariffs or bounties, will tend to employ themselves in those forms of production in which they can be used most effectively, *i.e.*, in which they will produce the largest amount of wealth. Left free to find their own level, that employment which engages them by higher profits and higher wages will be the employment which will enable them to contribute most to the aggregate production of wealth of the community. Just as individuals left free in the use of their productive powers will find, on the average, that their own greatest gain lies in that work which contributes most to the gain of the community, so, if there were absolute equality of competition amongst a group of nations, each nation would so employ its productive powers as to produce its maximum of wealth with its minimum of exertion. Thus, in proportion as one or more nations adopt protective measures, either in the shape of tax or bounty, the protected industries use an excessive amount of requisites of production in their work, and lessen the aggregate of wealth produced, damaging their own interests, and to a less extent the interests of other nations belonging to the industrial community. This is the theory of free trade stated in its broad principles. Now, with this theory, taken *in vacuo*, we have no quarrel; it is perfectly correct as a theory of exchange in an ideal industrial community. But, as a working principle of practical economics, it involves one important assumption.

Free Trade requires for its advantageous working a perfectly healthy condition of commerce, where the demand always keeps pace with the possibility of Supply; in a word, it assumes that whatever *can* be produced *will* be produced, and that whatever is produced is consumed. In such a condition it will be evident that any species of Protection will lessen the amount of possible production by increasing the average quantity of requisites of production packed in each Commodity, and will restrict the amount of Consumption. But in a diseased state of Commerce, where Under-consumption, acting by the pressure of Over-supply, has so congested the retail-system that an excessive amount of the requisites of production is already packed in each commodity, it by no means follows that a Protective System will have the same noxious result.

A protective tariff imposed in such a state so as to increase the average cost of making (*i.e.*, the average amount of uses of requisites of production) of each piece of goods, would act as a preventive check to that process whereby requisites of production formerly engaged in Making passed into Retailing. For the congestion of Retail trade was seen to have been brought about in the following manner:—A larger quantity of requisites of production existed than were economically required to produce the quantity of commodities the community would consent to consume. Since the amount of requisites of production which can be occupied in making cannot for any length of time exceed the minimum which the conditions of production require, while the work of trading can be easily distended so as to provide employment for any quantity of requisites of production, any excess of requisites of production which from time to time may occur in the making departments (whether by a fall off in consumption or by an application of more economic methods in manufacturing) is continually expelled from the making department and compelled to take refuge in the trading department, which, we have seen, becomes congested with excessive forms of capital and labour. In such a condition of affairs it is evident that any legislative restriction which might artificially increase the quantity of requisites of production whose use was required in making would to that extent act as a preventive of the further congestion of retail trade. In short, certain requisites of production, which would otherwise have passed on to increase the quantity of requisites of production engaged in retailing, will be kept employed in making.

To illustrate roughly, by figures, let us suppose that, in order to supply the current rate of consumption in a community, it is necessary that 9 x requisites of production be engaged in making and 1 x in retailing. Now, suppose that by saving, growth of population, and opening of new lands, 12 x requisites of production have come into existence. If this growth of the requisites of production has been coincident with a corresponding growth of consumption, all is well. But assume that the rate of consumption has remained the same, inducing that state of over-supply which is chronic in modern communities, what will happen? Under a condition of Free Trade internal competition will (as we have shown, Chapter VI.) force the excessive 2 x requisites of production into retailing until 3 x requisites of production are swallowed up in performing the work which could economically be done by 1 x. If, instead of conceding Free Trade, we assume a tariff which compels makers to devote themselves to kinds of making which require 11 x requisites of production in order to produce the same quantity of goods formerly produced by 9 x requisites of production, it is clear that, instead of the 2 x requisites of production engaging themselves in retail trade, they will be compelled to engage in making in order that the actual demand may be supplied. Thus, the only result of Protection would be that an excess of requisites of production would be employed in making instead of in retailing. In other words, we claim to have clearly shown that, in a state of depressed trade, a large amount of requisites of production is forced into retailing which is not there required, and which, however busily employed, performs no valuable service. The result of protective measures would, by providing employment for a larger quantity of requisites of production in the processes of making, prevent this unhealthy expansion of retail trade. If it be urged that the effect would only be to substitute waste in one point of the industrial machine for waste in another point, we admit the truth of this contention. The point on which we lay stress is simply this, that, in a condition of depressed trade, Protective measures do not inflict the damage which the orthodox Freetraders assign to them.

The theory of the Limiting Requisite set forth in Chapter VI. will, of course, suggest various practical considerations of importance to the largest class of the community, those whose sole requisite of production is labour. The question for them is how to keep labour in the position of limiting requisite. It is evident that so long as the quantity of labour offered for use exceeds the total required, the wages of labour will be kept at the minimum for which such quantity of labour will be supplied. To limit the available quantity of labour not absolutely but relatively to the quantity of labour required, will therefore be the interest of the labouring classes. This end they may achieve by the following means :—

a. By doing all in their power to increase the general consumption they will be increasing the quantity of the use of all the requisites of production in current demand. In ordinary circumstances, it has been seen, it is easier to increase the available amount of capital and natural agents than to increase the available amount of labour. Thus, every absolute increase of the quantity consumed in a community tends to strengthen the control of labour over production. If in a community there exists surplus labour to the smallest appreciable extent, say five per cent., ordinary wages are kept to a minimum. But if in such an industrial condition there was a desire to add ten per cent. to consumption, and therefore to the demand for the use of each requisite of production, it is clear that labour, being unable to supply more than five per cent. increase, would, from the difficulty and slowness of any further increase, be placed in the position of limiting requisite, and would take in wages the whole result of production, minus that fraction for which the owners of capital and natural agents would consent to use their possessions.

But though labour will theoretically be enabled at last to secure the full advantage of any such increase in consumption, it has been pointed out that the intricate and slow operation of such commercial movements will, in fact, divide the immediate benefit among the owners of all the requisites of production, as was illustrated by what occurred during the swollen consumption of the Franco-German war period. Any increase in general consumption will increase the total fund out of which profits, rent, wages are paid, and all will gain by such increase, though not in the same proportion.

β. Labour may mitigate the worst effect of under-consumption, without causing any increase in general consumption.

1. If the labourer has open to him an alternative method of subsistence, whether this be squatting on vacant land, workhouse accommodation, or facilities for emigration, it is universally admitted that such alternative measures the minimum of wages which he can receive for selling the use of his labour to the capitalist.

The effect of any of these alternatives is that the labourers will never accept lower wages for their labour than the equivalent of the best alternative open to them; for instance, if they would prefer the workhouse to ten shillings a week, then wages cannot fall below ten shillings a week, or if the workhouse accommodation were so improved that the average labourer regarded it as worth fifteen shillings a week, then wages could never fall below fifteen shillings a week.

Thus, labourers, if by legislative or other measures they can raise the standard of the alternative method of subsistence, can continually raise the minimum of wages. Nor is it true, as economists often maintain, that by so doing they are killing the goose with the golden eggs. Assuming that there is under-consumption, the effect of such increase would be simply to divert into the pockets of the labourers certain funds which would otherwise be wasted in an undue multiplication of the retailing classes.

2. It is also open to labourers by various methods to so limit their numbers as to keep themselves in the position of owners of the Limiting Requisite. What can be done in this way has recently been shown by the dock labourers. These labourers refused to work below a certain minimum price, and a general strike, that is to say, a withdrawal of the whole supply of labour, promptly put the labourers in the position of the requisite of production limiting production in that particular district and trade. This action issued in a general rise in the wages of the London dock labourers. So soon as labourers resolutely refuse to compete for work below a certain given hourly or weekly price, wages cannot fall below that point. What holds of the labourers of a single trade will here hold of the labourers of a Community or Nation. If the labourers of any nation are liable to have brought into the arena of competition a class of foreign labourers who will consent to work for less wages than the minimum to which they have been accustomed, it is evident that in any period of under-consumption the introduction of such foreigners will reduce the rate of wages to the point at which the labourers with the lowest standard of comfort will just consent to work. Thus the instinct which has led Americans and Australians to refuse to permit immigration of Chinese was a true instinct, and is justi-

fied by economic theory. Of course, if full economic demand existed, so that consumption kept pace with any possible increase of production, the competition of Chinese or other foreign labour would, as the economists urge, be harmless; for in this case the foreign labourers' wages would rise to the higher standard, instead of depressing the higher standard to its own. But it must not be forgotten that even in this case, supposing the new labour to be practically unlimited in quantity, it might put either capital or natural agents in the position of the requisite of production limiting production, and though the aggregate of wealth produced would be largely increased, a less share of this wealth would fall to the labourers.

What holds of Chinese immigration to America, of course holds also of the immigration of foreign paupers to this country. If German labourers will work for two shillings a day, the free admission of these will, assuming a continuance of under-consumption, eventually bring down English wages to this level. Thus, it is clearly for the interest of the English labourers to prevent, by legislation if necessary, such free influx of foreign labour as shall enable the quantity of labour demanded to be supplied at an unduly low rate of wages.

Although it may not be at first sight obvious, the same result will follow from any legal restriction of number of hours of labour, provided it be accompanied by absolute prohibition of imported labour. The effect of a law fixing the maximum hours of labour at eight per diem, instead of, say, ten, would be the same, so far as wages are concerned, as a law which expelled from the community one-fifth of the available labourers. Since each labourer will now only produce four-fifths of what he produced before (setting aside the vexed question of the effect of shorter hours upon the quality of labour), five labourers are now required where four were previously, and looking at the lowest kind of work, we must conclude that each of the five labourers has to be paid the same amount of wages as each of the four were paid before.

It is, however, necessary to bear in mind that an eight hours' bill must be universal. If otherwise (unless the nation enacting it isolated itself from all other nations by tariffs) the competition of other nations would undersell the eight hours' nation, ruin its capitalists, and so reduce the quantity of labour demanded as to force either a general emigration of the labourers, the repeal of the law, or its systematic and general evasion.

Assuming, however, that the eight hours' labour law is universal and that there is Under-consumption, the increased sum paid to labourers as demand for the use of labour will be deducted from the total of retail profits. Or, to put it otherwise, the increased number of labourers required for certain of the stages of production will be withdrawn from the number unnecessarily engaged (directly or indirectly) in retailing. Whilst, therefore, the total of production will not be affected, the aggregate of labour actually exerted will be reduced in the proportion of ten to eight. In any period of full demand it is evident that the aggregate produced would be reduced; in all such periods, therefore, it would be desirable to relax any limits that might be imposed restricting the hours of labour, unless it appeared that the advantages of increased leisure more than counterbalanced the loss of wages which in such periods would result.